Yanmar

YANMAR MARINE DIESEL ENGINES 4JHE, 4JH-TE, 4JH-HTE, 4JH-DTE

Service Manual

Yanmar

YANMAR MARINE DIESEL ENGINES 4JHE, 4JH-TE, 4JH-HTE, 4JH-DTE

Service Manual

ISBN/EAN: 9783954273447
Erscheinungsjahr: 2013
Erscheinungsort: Bremen, Deutschland

© maritimepress in Europäischer Hochschulverlag GmbH & Co. KG, Fahrenheitstr. 1, 28359 Bremen. Alle Rechte beim Verlag und bei den jeweiligen Lizenzgebern.

www.maritimepress.de | office@maritimepress.de

Bei diesem Titel handelt es sich um den Nachdruck eines historischen, lange vergriffenen Buches. Da elektronische Druckvorlagen für diese Titel nicht existieren, musste auf alte Vorlagen zurückgegriffen werden. Hieraus zwangsläufig resultierende Qualitätsverluste bitten wir zu entschuldigen.

YANMAR
SERVICE MANUAL

MARINE DIESEL ENGINE

MODELS
4JHE
4JH-TE
4JH-HTE
4JH-DTE

FOREWORD

This service manual has been compiled for engineers engaged in sales, service, inspection and maintenance. Accordingly, descriptions of the construction and functions of the engine are emphasized in this manual while items which should already be common knowledge are omitted.

One characteristic of a marine diesel engine is that its performance in a vessel is governed by its applicability to the vessel's hull construction and its steering system.

Engine installation, fitting out and propeller selection have a substantial effect on the performance of the engine and the vessel. Moreover, when the engine runs unevenly or when trouble occurs, it is essential to check a wide range of operating conditions—such as installation on the hull and suitability of the ship's piping and propeller—and not just the engine itself. To get maximum performance from this engine, you should completely understand its functions, construction and capabilities, as well as proper use and servicing.

Use this manual as a handy reference in daily inspection and maintenance, and as a text for engineering guidance.

Models 4JH(B)E · 4JH-T(B)E
4JH-HT(B)E · 4JH-DT(B)E

CHAPTER 1 GENERAL
1. Exterior Views 1-1
2. Specifications 1-4
3. Construction. 1-5
4. Performance Curves 1-6
5. Engine Cross Section 1-10
6. Dimensions. 1-11
7. Piping Diagrams. 1-15
8. Parts Interchangeability. 1-18

CHAPTER 2 BASIC ENGINE PARTS
1. Cylinder Block 2-1
2. Cylinder Liners 2-4
3. Cylinder Head. 2-6
4. Piston and Piston Pins. 2-13
5. Connecting Rod. 2-17
6. Crankshaft and Main Bearing 2-20
7. Camshaft and Tappets. 2-23
8. Timing Gear 2-26
9. Flywheel and Housing. 2-28

CHAPTER 3 FUEL INJECTION EQUIPMENT
1. Fuel Supply System 3-1
2. Disassembly, Reassembly and Inspection
   of Governor. 3-9
3. Disassembly, Reassembly and Inspection
   of Fuel Injection Pump. 3-18
4. Adjustment of Fuel Injection
   Pump and Governor 3-28
5. Automatic Advancing Timer 3-34
6. Fuel Feed Pump 3-36
7. Fuel Injection Nozzle 3-38
8. Troubleshooting 3-42
9. Fuel Injection Pump Service Data 3-44
10. Tools 3-45
11. Fuel Filter 3-47
12. Fuel Tank (Optional) 3-48
13. Design Change of Fuel Piping Line 3-49

CHAPTER 4 INTAKE AND EXHAUST SYSTEM
1. Intake and Exhaust System 4-1
2. Intake Silencer 4-4
3. Intake Manifold. 4-5
4. Turbocharger 4-6
5. Mixing Elbow 4-21
6. Breather. 4-22

CHAPTER 5 LUBRICATION SYSTEM
1. Lubrication System 5-1
2. Lube Oil Pump 5-3
3. Lube Oil Filter 5-6
4. Oil Pressure Control Valve. 5-8
5. Lube Oil Cooler. 5-9
6. Piston Cooling Nozzle. 5-11
7. Rotary Waste Oil Pump (Optional) 5-12

CHAPTER 6 COOLING WATER SYSTEM
1. Cooling Water System. 6-1
2. Sea Water Pump. 6-4
3. Fresh Water Pump .6-7
4. Heat Exchanger 6-10
5. Pressure Cap and Sub Tank 6-12
6. Thermostat. 6-14
7. Kingston Cock (Optional) 6-16
8. Sea Water Filter (Optional) 6-17
9. Bilge Pump and Bilge Strainer (Optional) 6-18

CHAPTER 7 REDUCTION AND REVERSING GEAR
Marine gear model KBW 20 and 21
1. Construction. 7-1
2. Installation 7-6
3. Inspection and Servicing 7-7
4. Operation and Maintenance 7-8
5. Disassembly 7-13
6. Reassembly. 7-17
7. Special Tools. 7-23

Marine gear model KM4A, (Angle drive)
1. Construction 7-24
2. Shifting Device 7-28
3. Inspection and Servicing. 7-33
4. Special Tools 7-43
5. Disassembly 7-45
6. Reassembly 7-53

CHAPTER 8 REMOTE CONTROL
1. Remote Control System 8-1
2. Remote Control Installation. 8-2
3. Remote Control Inspection 8-5
4. Remote Control Adjustment 8-6

CHAPTER 9 ELECTRICAL SYSTEM
1. Electrical System 9-1
2. Battery 9-6
3. Starter Motor 9-9
4. Alternator 9-20
5. Instrument Panel and Wiring Codes 9-30
6. Warning Devices 9-35
7. Air Heater (Optional) 9-38
8. Electric Type Engine Stop Device (Optional). . . .9-39
9. Tachometer 9-41
10. Alternator 12V/80A (Optional) 9-44

CHAPTER 10 DISASSEMBLY AND REASSEMBLY
1. Disassembly and Reassembly Precautions 10-1
2. Disassembly and Reassembly Tools 10-2
3. Disassembly and Reassembly 10-9
4. Bolt/nut Tightening Torque 10-32
5. Test Running 10-33

Printed in Japan
0000 A0 A1647

CHAPTER 1
GENERAL

1. Exterior Views 1-1
2. Specifications 1-4
3. Construction. 1-5
4. Performance Curves 1-6
5. Engine Cross Section .1-10
6. Dimensions. 1-11
7. Piping Diagrams. 1-15
8. Parts Interchangeability. 1-18

Chapter 1 General
1. Exterior Views   4JH Series

1. Exterior Views

1-1 4JHE

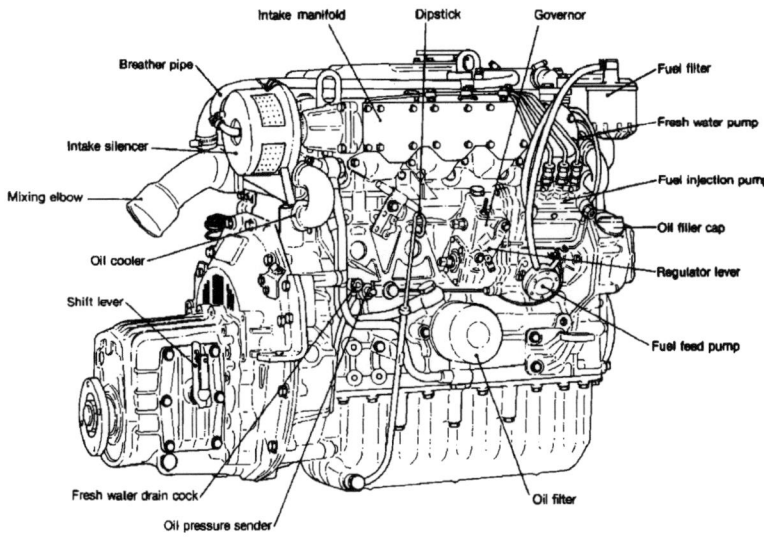

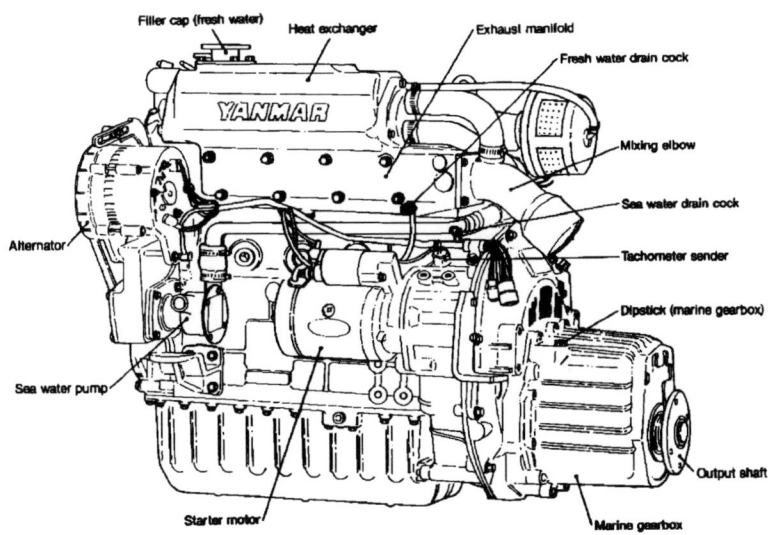

Chapter 1 General
1. Exterior Views

4JH Series

1-2 4JH-TE

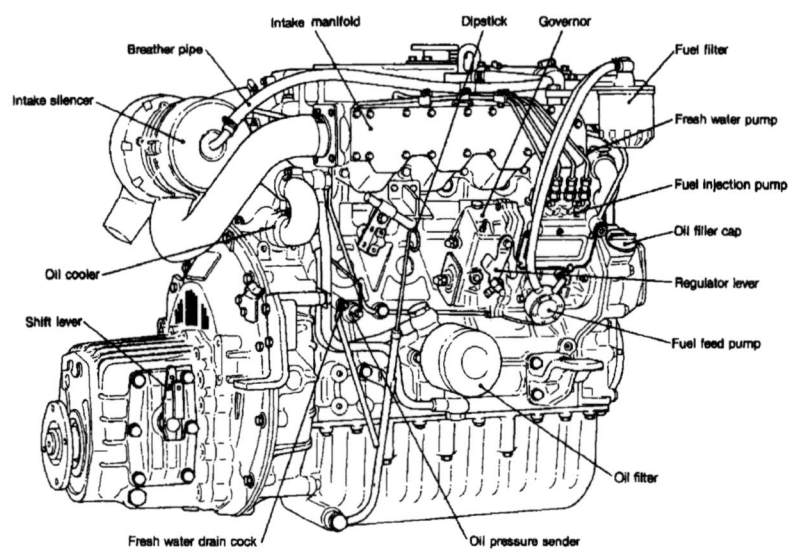

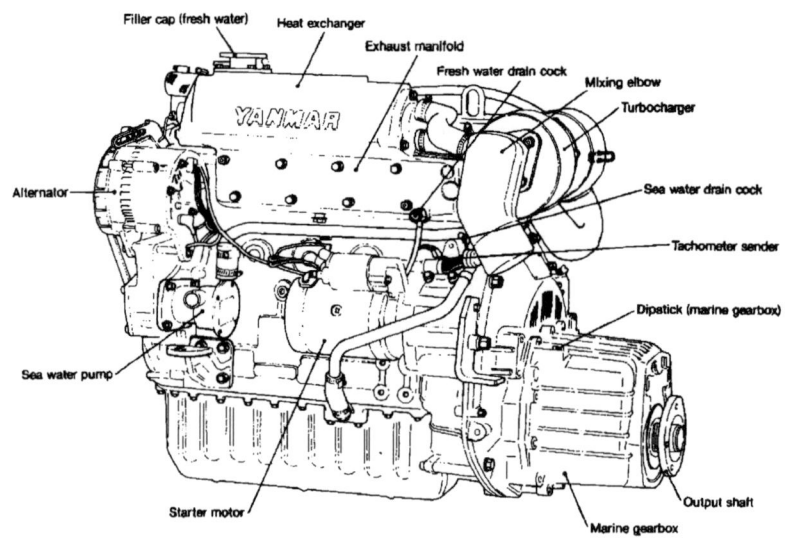

Chapter 1 General
1. Exterior Views

1-3 4JH-HTE & 4JH-DTE

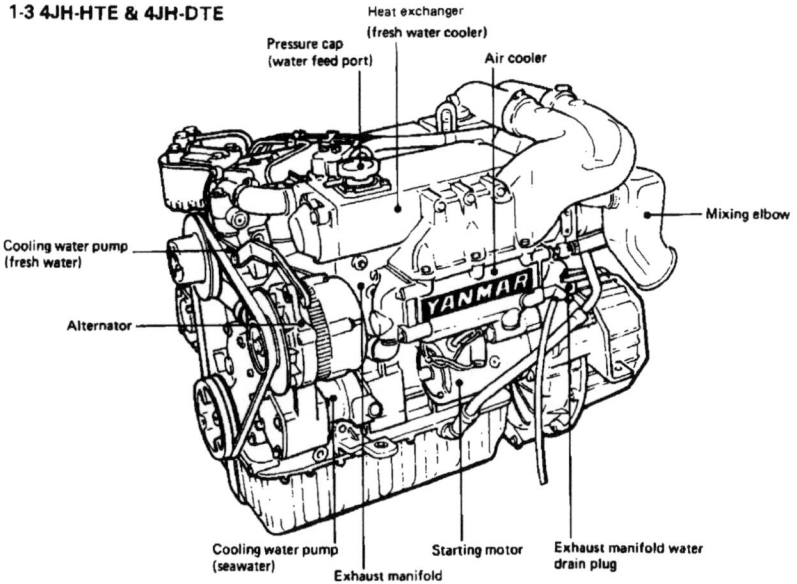

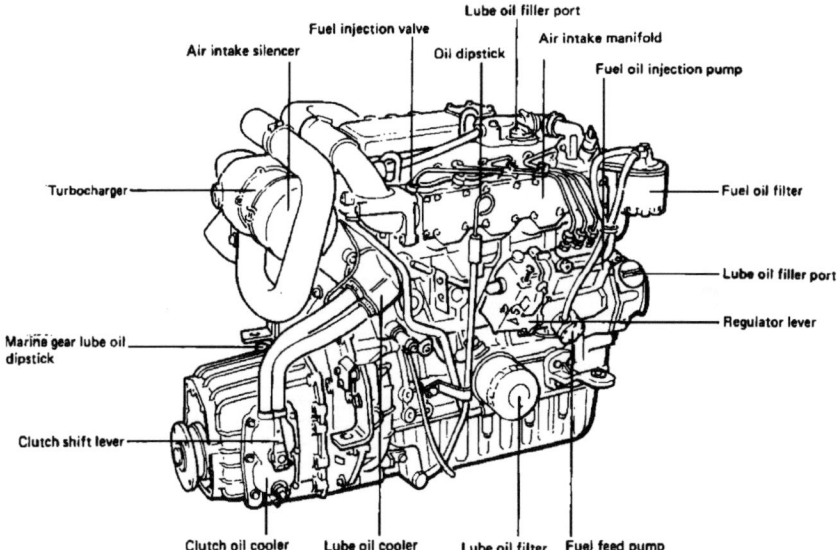

Chapter 1 General
2. Specifications

4JH Series

2. Specifications

Model			4JHE	4JH-TE	4JH-HTE	4JH-DTE
Type			Vertical 4-cycle water cooled diesel engine			
Combustion system			Direct Injection			
Aspiration			Normal aspiration	Exhaust gas turbine turbocharger	Exhaust gas turbine turbocharger with intercooler	
Number of cylinders			4			
Bore x stroke		mm (in.)	78 x 86 (3.07 x 3.39)			
Displacement		ℓ (cu.in.)	1.644 (100.33)			
One hour rating output (DIN62708)	Output/crankshaft speed	HP/rpm (kW/rpm)	44/3600 (32.4/3600)	55/3600 (40.5/3600)	66/3600 (48.6/3600)	77/3600 (56.7/3600)
	Brake mean effective pressure	Kg/cm^2 (lb./in.^{2})	6.69 (95.15)	8.36 (118.91)	10.0 (142.20)	11.7 (166.37)
	Piston speed	m/sec. (ft./sec.)	10.3 (33.79)	10.3 (33.79)	10.3 (33.79)	10.3 (33.79)
Continuous rating output (DIN6270A)	Output/crankshaft speed	HP/rpm (kW/rpm)	40/3500 (29.5/3500)	50/3500 (36.8/3500)	60/3500 (44.2/3500)	70/3500 (51.5/3500)
	Brake mean effective pressure	kg/cm^2 (lb./in.^{2})	6.26 (89.04)	7.82 (111.23)	9.39 (133.53)	11.0 (156.42)
	Piston speed	m/sec. (ft./sec)	10.0 (32.81)	10.0 (32.81)	10.0 (32.81)	10.0 (32.81)
Compression ratio			17.8	16.2	15.9	15.9
Fire order			$180°\quad 180°\quad 180°\quad 180°$ $1 - 3 - 4 - 2 - 1$			
Fuel injection pump			Bosch in-line type YPES-CL			
Fuel injection timing (FID)		degree	$12° \pm 1°$ bTDC (*$9° \pm 1°$)	$12° \pm 1°$ bTDC	$12° \pm 1°$ bTDC	$12° \pm 1°$ bTDC
Fuel injection pressure		kg/cm^2 (lb./in.^{2})	200 ±5 (2844 ±71)			
Fuel Injection nozzles			Hole type			
Direction of rotation	Crankshaft		Counter-clockwise viewed from starn			
	Propeller shaft (Forward)		Clockwise viewed from stern			
Power take off			At flywheel side			
Cooling system			Constant high temperature fresh water cooling Fresh water: Centrifugal pump Sea water: Rubber impeller pump			
Lubrication system			Forced lubrication with trochoid pump			
Starting system	Starting motor		DC 12V, 1.8kW			
	AC generator		12V, 55A			
Turbocharger	Type			RHB52 (IHI)	RHB52HW (IHI)	
	Model			MY29	MY31	MY34
	Cooling system			Air cooling	Water cooling	
Air cooler system	Type				Sea-water cooled, Plate fin type	Sea-water cooled, Corrugated fin type
	Radiation area	m^2 (In.^{2})			0.76 (1178)	0.67 (1038)
Clutch	Model		KBW20		KBW21	KBW21
	Type		Constant mesh gear with multiple friction disc clutch			
	Reduction ratio (Forward/Reverse)		2.17/3.06, 2.62/3.06, 3.28/3.06			2.17/3.06, 2.62/3.06
	Propeller speed DIN6270A rating (Forward/Reverse)		1615/1145, 1336/1145, 1068/1145			1615/1145, 1336/1145
	Lubricating oil capacity Effect/max	ℓ (cu.in.)	0.15/1.2 (9.15/73.22)			
	Clutch weight	kg (lb.)	26 (57.33)		30 (66.15)	30 (66.15)
Dimensions	Overall length	mm (in.)	906.3 (35.68)		906.3 (35.68)	906.3 (35.68)
	Overall width	mm (in)	561 (22.09)		561 (22.09)	561 (22.09)
	Overall height	mm (in.)	659 (25.94)		668 (26.30)	668 (26.30)
Engine weight with clutch (dry)		kg (lb.)	226 (498)	232 (511)	246 (542)	246 (542)
Lubricating oil capacity Effect/max.		ℓ (cu.In.)	3.0/6.5 (183.06/396.63)			
Cooling water capacity (Fresh water)	Fresh water tank	ℓ (cu.In.)	6.0 (366.12)			
	Sub tank	ℓ (cu.In.)	0.8 (48.82)			

Note: *Applicable engine number #/E 00101 ~ 00574

1-4

Chapter 1 General
3. Construction

3. Construction

ENGINE MODEL		4JH	4JH-TE	4JH-HTE	4JH-DTE
Group	Part	Construction			
Engine Proper	Cylinder block	Integrally-cast water jacket and crankcase			
	Cylinder liner	Dry sleeve			
	Timing gear case	Cast aluminum			
	Oil sump	Cast aluminum, oil pan			
	Main bearings	Hanger-type bearings supports			
	Engine feet	Cylinder block and Flywheel mounting side			
Intake/Exhaust, Valve Drive	Cylinder head	Integrally-cast type, jet cooling between valves, Intake/exhaust valve seat inserts			
	Intake/exhaust valves	Mushroom shaped, seat angle: Intake: 120° Exhaust: 90°			
	Intake manifold	Aluminum diecast Integral			
	Exhaust manifold	Water cooled integral with water tank			
	Air cooler			Plate fin type	Corrugated fin type
	Turbocharger	—	IHI RHB52 exhaust gas turbo	IHI RHB52HW exhaust gas turbo, Water cooled type.	
	Valve drive	Overhead valve push rod rocker arm system			
	Timing gear	Helical gear			
Main Moving Parts	Crankshaft	Stamped forging			
	Flywheel	Cast iron static balance with ring gear			
	Pistons	Cast aluminum, oval type			
	Piston rings	2 compression rings, 1 oil ring			
	Piston pin	Floating type			
	Connecting rod	Forged steel			
	Crank pin bushings	Aluminum bushings			
Lube Oil System	Lube oil pump	Trochoid type			
	Oil filter	Full flow paper element cartridge type			
	Oil cooler	Sea water cooled pipe type		Sea water cooled multi-pipe type	
	Control valve	Cylindrical type with external adjusting shims			
Cooling Water System	Fresh water pump	V-pulley driven, centrifugal type			
	Sea water pump	Gear driven, rubber Impeller type			
	Thermostat	Wax pellet type			
	Fresh water cooler	Multi-tube type integral with exhaust manifold			
Bilge	Bilge pump	Electric			
Fuel Injection Equipment	Fuel injection pump	YANMAR YPES-CL type integral with governor			
	Fuel injection nozzles	Hole type			
	Fuel feed pump	Diaphragm type			
	Fuel filter	Paper element cartridge type			
Governor	Governor	Centrifugal all-speed mechanical type			
Remote Control Equipment	Engine speed & marine gearbox	Single control lever type with push-pull cable			
Starting Equipment	Electric starter	DC 12V, 1.8kW starter motor			
	Generator	12V, 55A with built-in IC regulator			
Marine Gearbox	Clutch	Multi-disc mechanical wet type			
	Reduction gear	Helical gear constant mesh type			

4. Performance Curves

4-1 4JHE

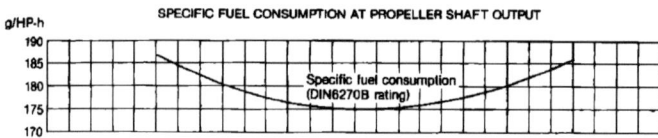

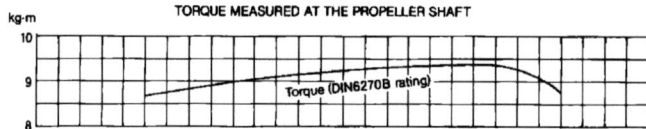

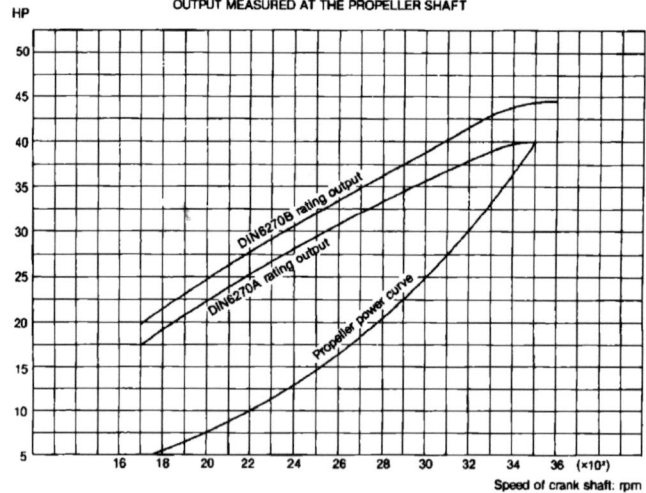

THE ENGINE FLYWHEEL OUTPUT IS APPROX. 3% HIGHER

Chapter 1 General
4. Performance Curves

4JH Series

4-2 4JH-TE

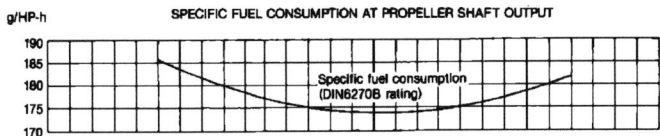

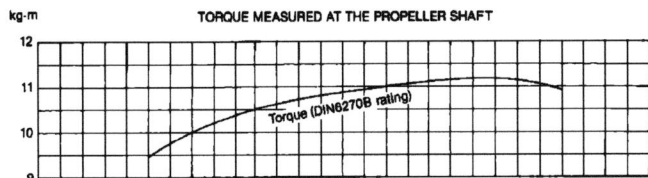

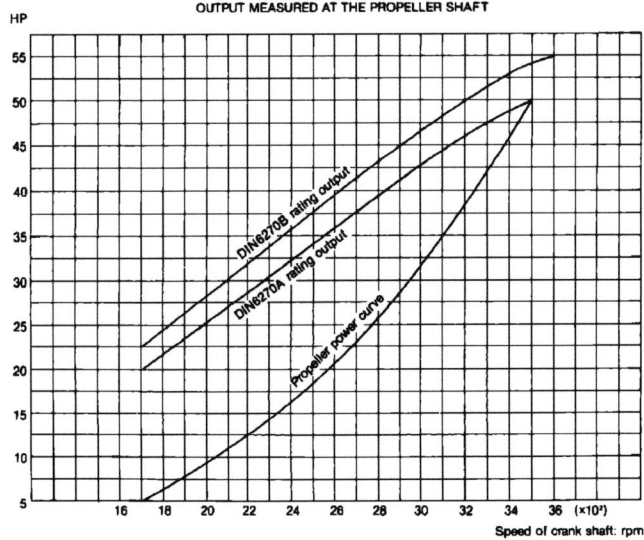

THE ENGINE FLYWHEEL OUTPUT IS APPROX. 3% HIGHER

Chapter 1 General
4. Performance Curves _____ *4JH Series*

4-3 4JH-HTE

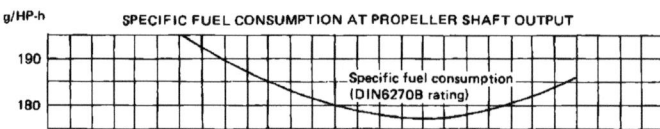

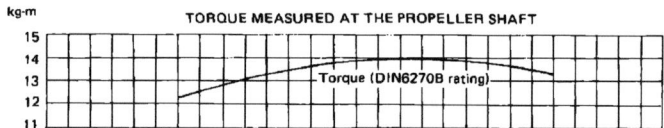

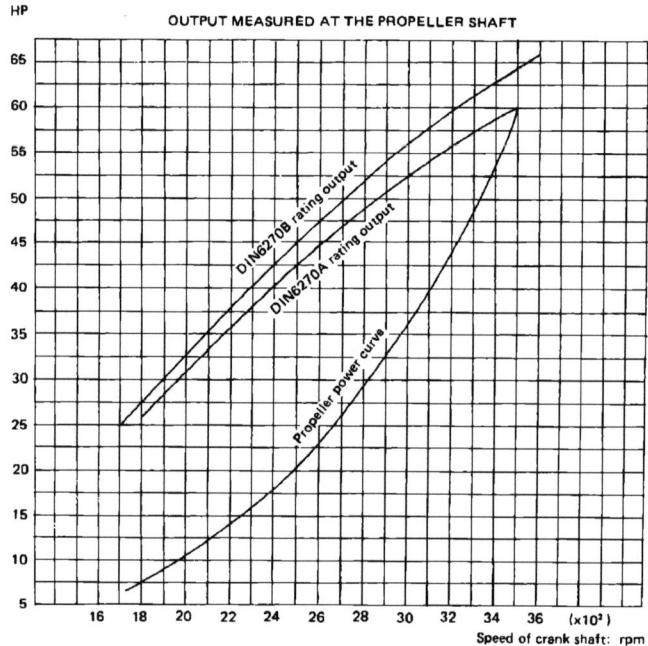

THE ENGINE FLYWHEEL OUTPUT IS APPROX, 3% HIGHER.

Chapter 1 General
4. Performance Curves — *4JH Series*

4-4 4JH-DTE

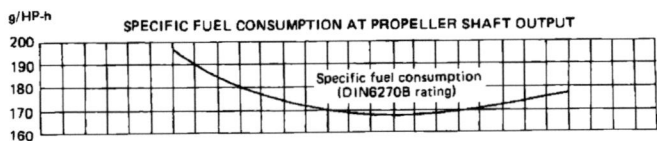

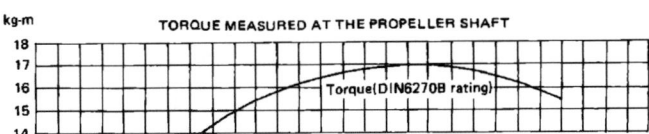

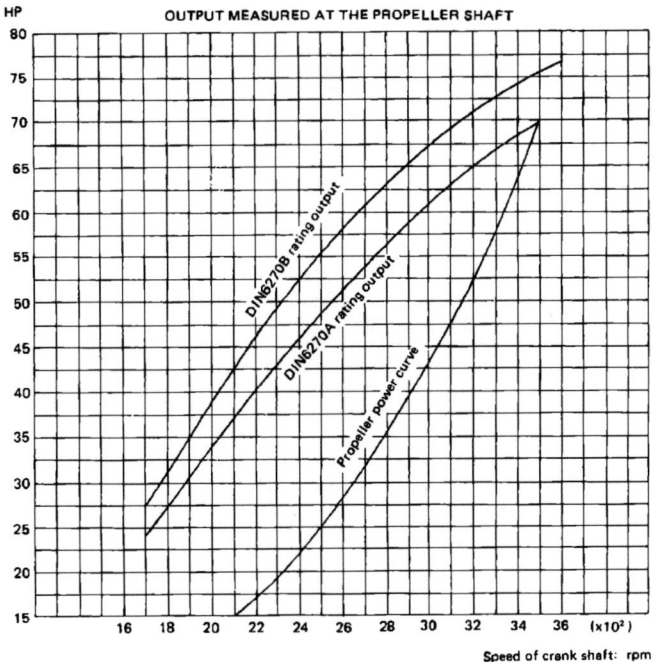

THE ENGINE FLYWHEEL OUTPUT IS APPROX. 3% HIGHER.

5. Engine Cross Section

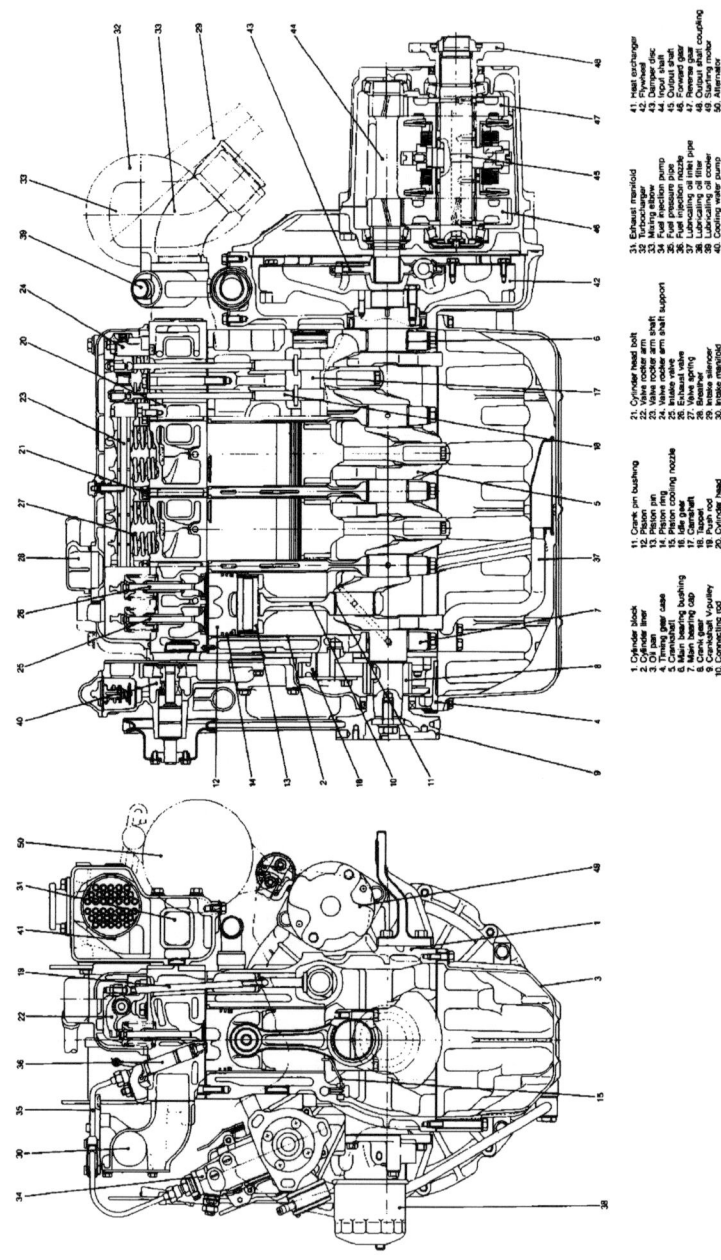

1. Cylinder block
2. Cylinder liner
3. Oil pan
4. Timing gear case
5. Crankshaft
6. Main bearing bushing
7. Crank gear
8. Cam gear
9. Crankshaft V-pulley
10. Connecting rod
11. Crank pin bushing
12. Piston
13. Piston pin
14. Piston ring
15. Piston cooling nozzle
16. Fuel injection nozzle
17. Camshaft
18. Tappet
19. Push rod
20. Cylinder head
21. Cylinder head bolt
22. Valve rocker arm
23. Valve rocker arm shaft
24. Valve rocker arm shaft support
25. Intake valve
26. Exhaust valve
27. Valve spring
28. Breather
29. Intake silencer
30. Intake manifold
31. Exhaust manifold
32. Turbocharger
33. Mixing elbow
34. Fuel injection pump
35. Fuel pressure pipe
36. Fuel injection nozzle
37. Lubricating oil inlet pipe
38. Lubricating oil filter
39. Lubricating oil cooler
40. Cooling water pump
41. Heat exchanger
42. Flywheel
43. Damper disc
44. Input shaft
45. Output shaft
46. Forward gear
47. Reverse gear
48. Output shaft coupling
49. Starting motor
50. Alternator

6. Dimensions

6-1 4JHE

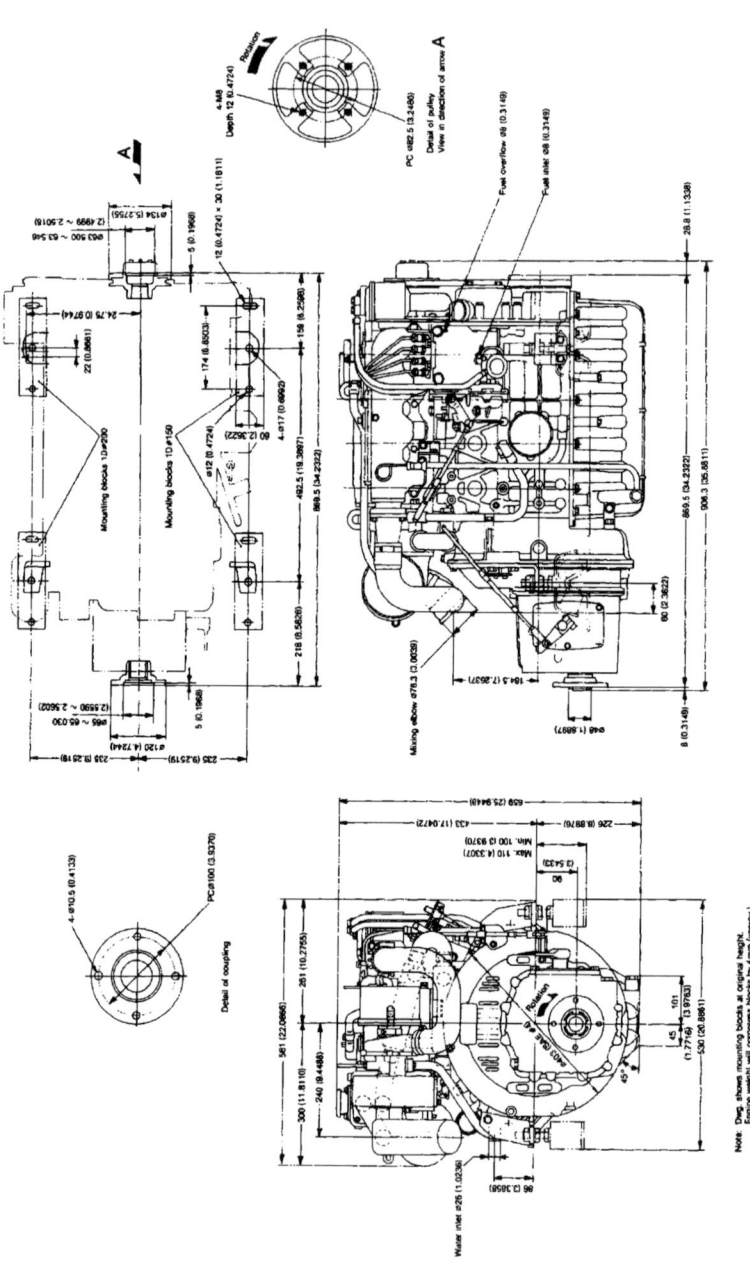

6-3 4JH-HTE

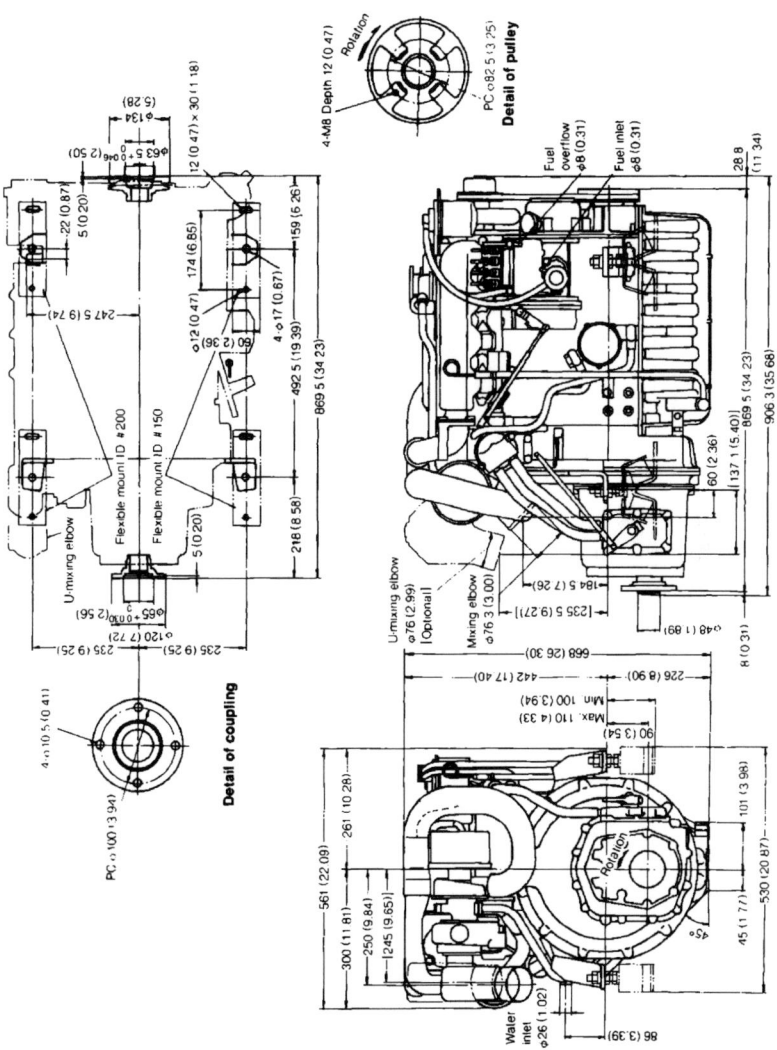

Chapter 1 General
6. Dimensions

6-4 4JH-DTE

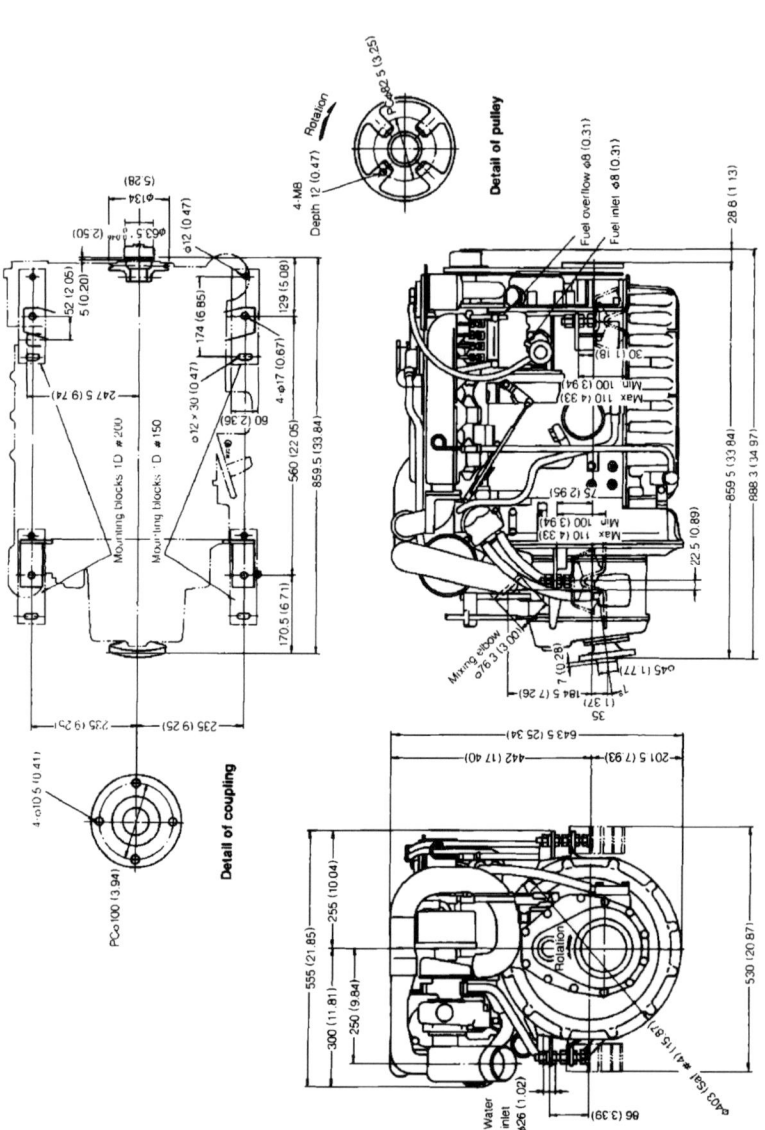

1-14

Chapter 1 General
7. Piping Diagrams _____ 4JH Series

7. Piping Diagrams

7-1 4JHE

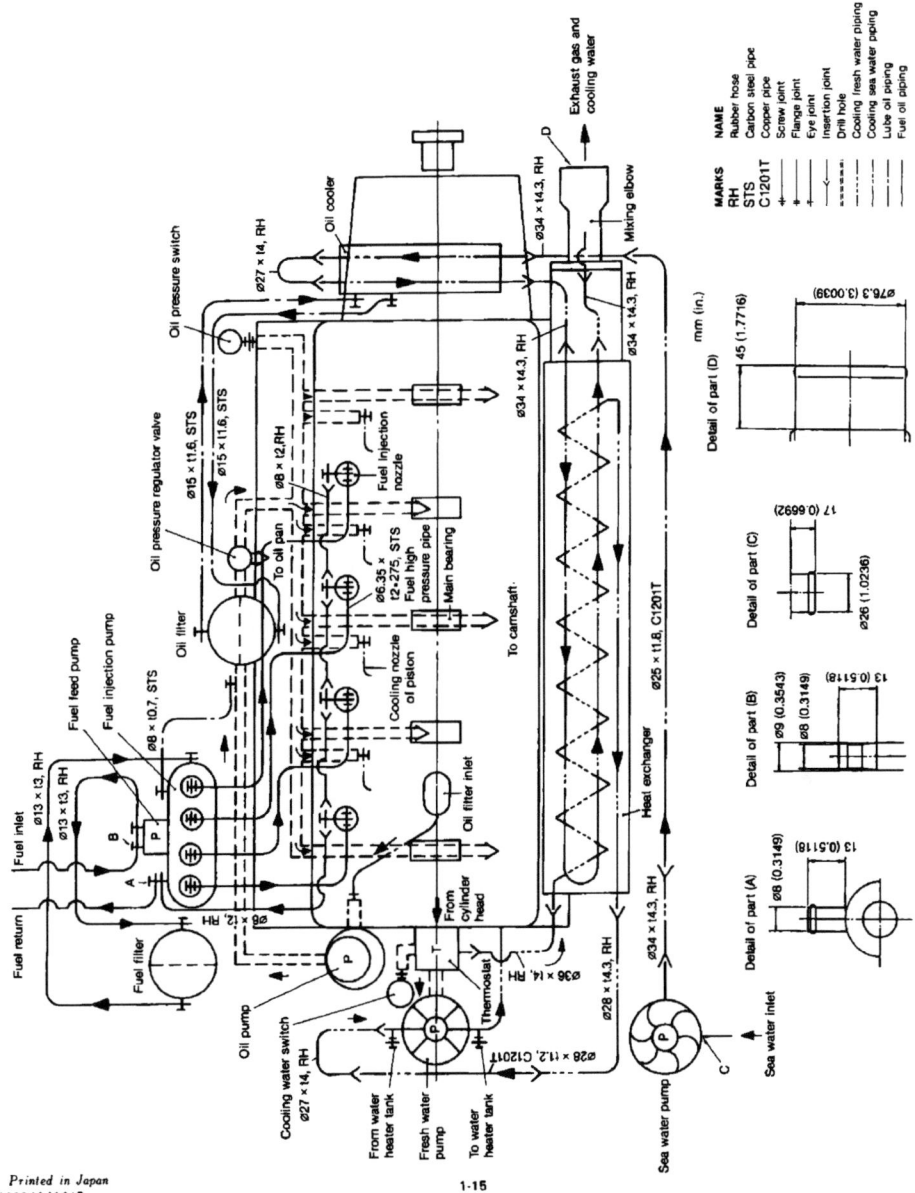

Chapter 1 General
7. Piping Diagrams _____ *4JH Series*

7-2 4JH-TE

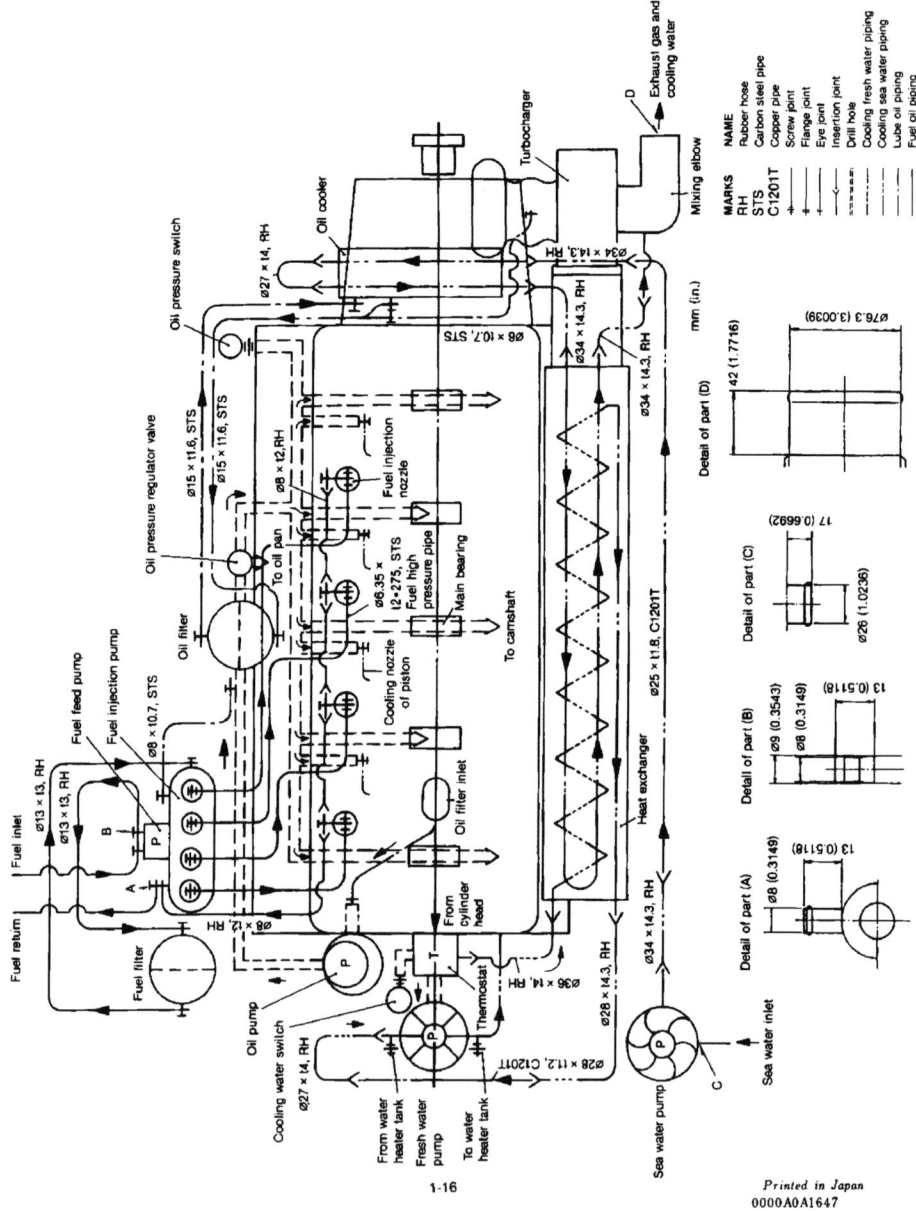

7-3 4JH-HTE & 4JH-DT(B)E

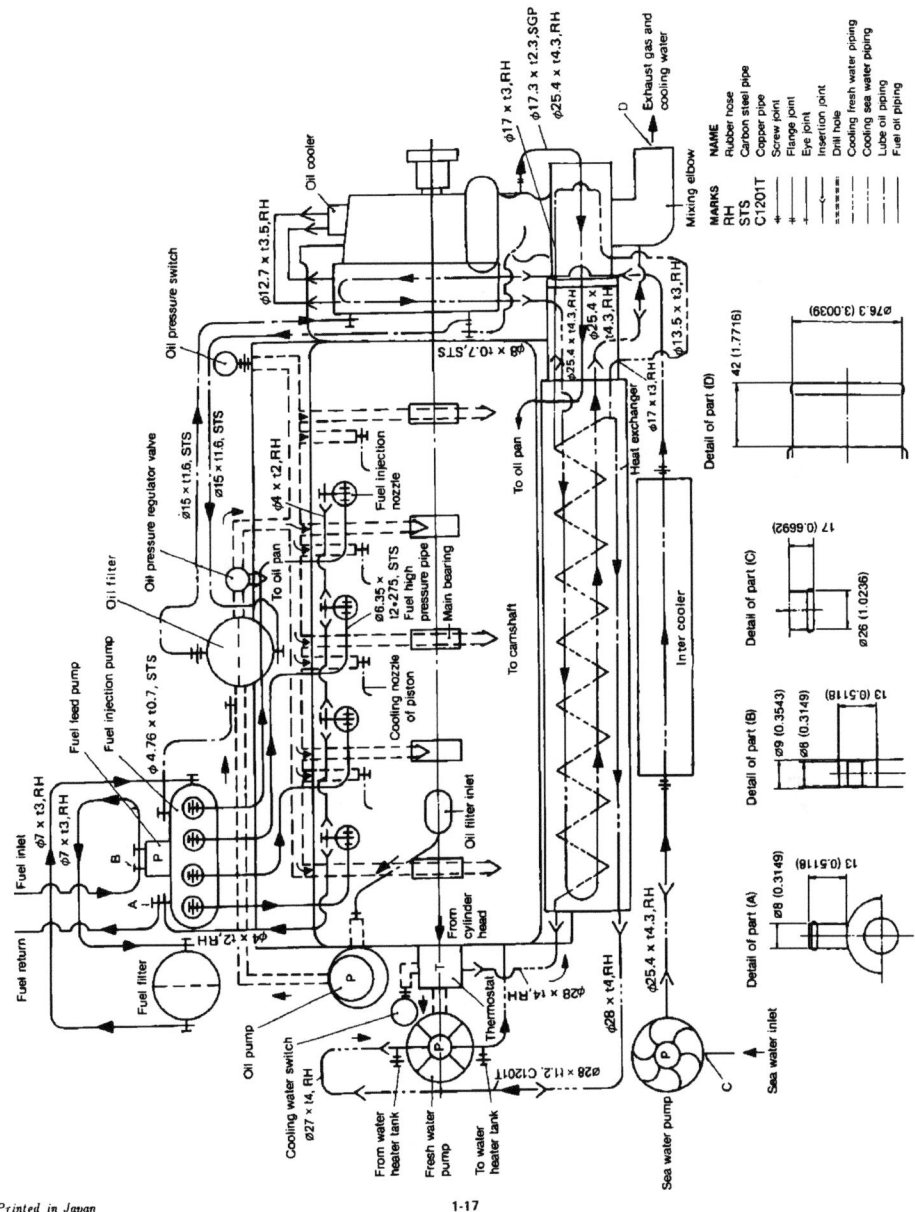

8. Parts Interchangeability

4JH-Series Parts Interchangeability (Cylinder Head Assembly, Piston and FIE)

IMPORTANT:
There is no interchangeability between the old type and the new type parts.
To ensure the parts interchangeability among the 4JH series engines, be sure to change all the relative parts as follows.

CHANGE PARTS			4JHE	4JH-TE	4JH-HTE	4JH-DTE	Note
1) Cylinder Head Ass'y	Old type	Part code: Swirl radio: Identification mark:	729470-11700 2.25 1	⇩	729474-11700 2.0 5	✕	Cylinder Head Applicable ENG. model I.D. mark
	New type	Part code: Swirl radio: Identification mark:	729470-11701 2.8 SL	729474-11701 2.0 SG	⇩	⇩	
2) Piston	Old type	Part code: Identification mark:	129400-22020 1	129472-22010 2	129474-22010 5	✕	Piston Applicable ENG. model I.D. mark
	New type	Part code: Identification mark:	129400-22021 A	129472-22011 B	129474-22010 C (only changed I.D. mark.)	⇩	
3)-1 Automatic Timer Ass'y (Automatic Advancing Timer)	Old type	Part code: Advanced angle: Cam. deg. Identification mark:	729470-54101 5.5 JH-A1	729472-54101 3.5 JH-B0	729499-54100 2.5 JH-C0	✕	Automatic Timer Applicable ENG. model I.D. mark
	New type	Part code: Advanced angle: Cam. deg. Identification mark:	729100-54100 4 TN-A0	729499-54100 2.5 JH-C0	⇩	⇩	
3)-2 Fuel Injection Nozzle A'ssy	Old type	Part code: Identification mark: Nozzle Identification mark:	729470-53101 D 158P244J1	729472-53100 D 150P29AJ0	729499-53100 D 146P285J1	✕	Nozzle holder Nozzle Nozzle body Applicable ENG. model I.D. mark
	New type	Part code: Identification mark: Nozzle Identification mark:	129470-53102 F 158P244J2	729499-53102 G 140P255J2	⇩	⇩	
3)-3 Fuel Return Pipe	Old type	Part code: Length:	129470-59550 90mm	⇩	⇩	✕	Fuel Return Pipe
	New type	Part code: Length:	121250-59550 120mm				
3)-4 Fuel Injection Pipe (Pump to Nozzle)	Old type	Part code: (No. 1 Cylinder) (No. 2 Cylinder) (No. 3 Cylinder) (No. 4 Cylinder) Size: Inner dia, Length, Identification mark:	129470-59810 129470-59820 129470-59830 129470-59840 ⌀1.8 400mm None	⇩	129499-59810 129499-59820 129499-59830 129499-59840 ⌀2.0 400mm None	✕	Fuel Injection Pipe No.1 No.2 No.3 No.4
	New type	Part code: (No. 1 Cylinder) (No. 2 Cylinder) (No. 3 Cylinder) (No. 4 Cylinder) Size: Inner dia, Length, Identification mark:	129470-59811 129470-59821 129470-59831 129470-59841 ⌀1.8 400mm 18	⇩	129499-59811 129499-59821 129499-59831 129499-59841 ⌀2.0 400mm 20	⇩	

Applicable Engine Model and Engine Number:
- 4JHE, E/#01001 and after (Jun., '2185 YANMAR Plant)
- 4JH-TE, E/#11001 and after (Jun., '2185 YANMAR Plant)
- 4JH-HTE, E/#21001 and after (Jun., '2185 YANMAR Plant)
- 4JH-DTE, E/#30101 and after (Jun., '2185 YANMAR Plant)

CHAPTER 2

INSPECTION AND SERVICING OF BASIC ENGINE PARTS

1. Cylinder Block 2-1
2. Cylinder Liners 2-4
3. Cylinder Head. 2-6
4. Piston and Piston Pins. 2-13
5. Connecting Rod. 2-17
6. Crankshaft and Main Bearing 2-20
7. Camshaft and Tappets. 2-23
8. Timing Gear 2-26
9. Flywheel and Housing. 2-28

Chapter 2 Basic Engine
1. Cylinder Block
4JH Series

1. Cylinder Block

The cylinder block is thin-skinned, (low-weight), short skirt type with rationally placed ribs. The side walls are wave shaped to maximize ridigity for strength and low noise.

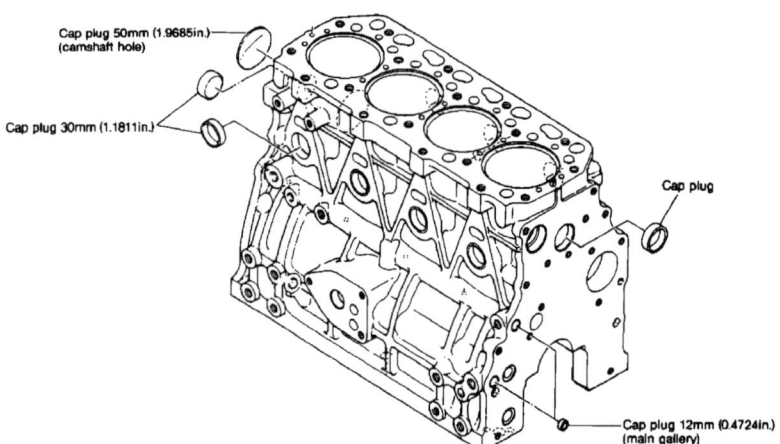

Cap plug 50mm (1.9685in.) (camshaft hole)
Cap plug 30mm (1.1811in.)
Cap plug
Cap plug 12mm (0.4724in.) (main gallery)

1-1 Inspection of parts

Make a visual inspection to check for cracks on engines that have frozen up, overturned or otherwise been subjected to undue stress. Perform a color check on any portions that appear to be cracked, and replace the cylinder block if the crack is not repairable.

1-2 Cleaning of oil holes

Clean all oil holes, making sure that none are clogged up and the blind plugs do not come off.

Color check kit Part code No. 97550-004560	Quantity
Penetrant	1
Developer	2
Cleaner	3

1-3 Color check procedure

(1) Clean the area to be inspected.
(2) Color check kit
The color check test kit consists of an aerosol cleaner, penetrant and developer.
(3) Clean the area to be inspected with the cleaner.
Either spray the cleaner on directly and wipe, or wipe the area with a cloth moistened with cleaner.
(4) Spray on red penetrant
After cleaning, spray on the red penetrant and allow 5 ~ 10 minutes for penetration. Spray on more red penetrant if it dries before it has been able to penetrate.
(5) Spray on developer
Remove any residual penetrant on the surface after the penetrant has penetrated, and spray on the developer.
If there are any cracks in the surface, red dots or a red line will appear several minutes after the developer dries.
Hold the developer 300 ~ 400mm (11.8110 ~ 15.7480in.) away from the area being inspected when spraying, making sure to coat the surface uniformly.
(6) Clean the surface with the cleaner.

NOTE: *Without fail, read the instructions for the color check kit before use.*

Chapter 2 Basic Engine
1. Cylinder Block

4JH Series

1-4 Replacement of cup plugs

Step No.	Description	Procedure	Tool or material used
1.	Clean and remove grease from the hole into which the cup plug is to be driven. (Remove scale and sealing material previously applied.)	Remove foreign materials with a screw driver or saw blade.	•Screw driver or saw blade •Thinner
2.	Remove grease from the cup plug.	Visually check the nick around the plug.	•Thinner
3.	Apply Threebond No. 4 to the seat surface where the plug is to be driven in.	Apply over the whole outside of the plug.	•Threebond No. 4
4.	Insert the plug into the hole.	Insert the plug so that it sits correctly.	
5.	Place a driving tool on the cup plug and drive it in using a hammer.	Drive in the plug parallel to the seating surface.	•Driving tool •Hammer

2 ~ 3mm (0.0787 ~ 0.1181in.)

3mm (0.1181in.)   100mm (3.9370in.)

*Using the special tool, drive the cup plug to a depth where the edge of the plug is 2mm (0.0787in.) below the cylinder surface.

mm (in.)

Plug dia.	d	D
ø12	ø11.9 ~ 12.0 (ø0.4685 ~ 0.4724)	ø20 (ø0.7874)
ø30	ø29.9 ~ 30.0 (ø1.1770 ~ 1.8110)	ø40 (ø1.5748)

1-5 Cylinder bore measurement

Measure the bore diameter with a cylinder gauge at the positions shown in the figure.
Replace the cylinder bore when the measured value exceeds the wear limit. Measurement must be done at least at 3 positions as shown in the figure, namely, top, middle and bottom positions in both directions along the crankshaft rotation and crankshaft center lines.

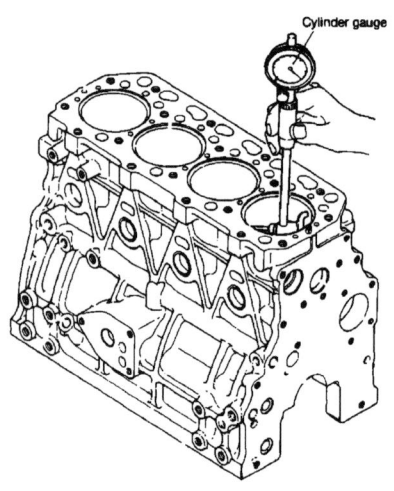
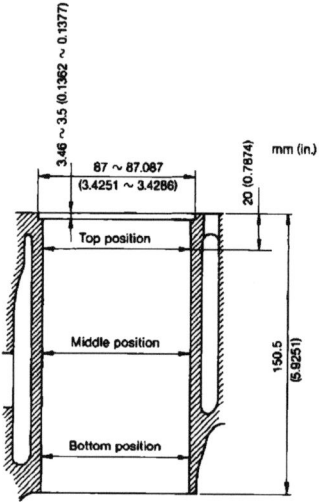
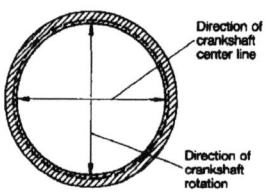

	Standard	Wear limit
Cylinder bore dia.	ø82.00 ~ 82.03 (3.2283 ~ 3.2295)	ø82.06 (3.2307)
Cylinder roundness	0 ~ 0.01 (0 ~ 0.0004)	0.02 (0.0008)

mm (in.)

2. Cylinder Liners

2-1 Measuring cylinder liners

Measure the inner diameter of each cylinder with a cylinder gauge and replace the cylinder liner if it exceeds the wear limit.

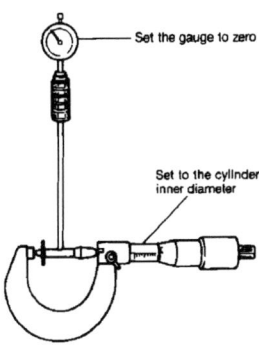

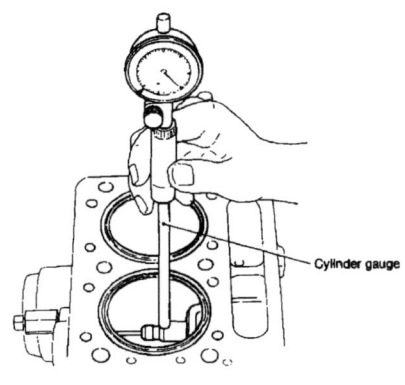

2-2 Inserting cylinder liners

Coat the outside of the liner with oil, and insert lightly by hand. Do not tap with a wooden hammer as this may deform the liner.

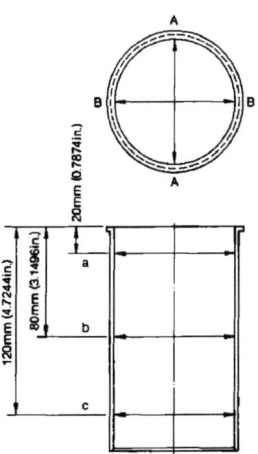

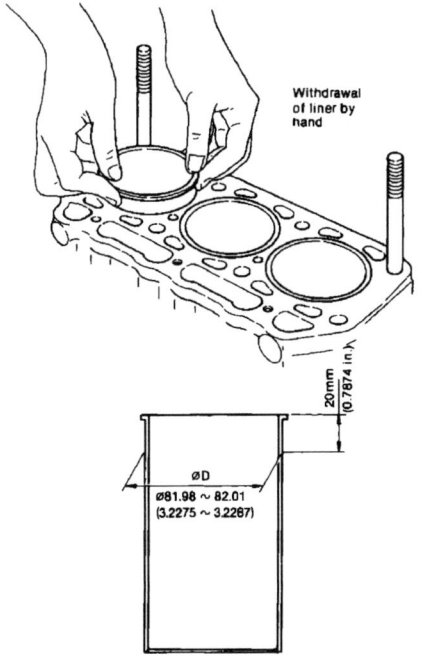

mm (in.)

	Standard	Wear limit
Cylinder liner	ø78.00 ~ 78.03 (ø3.0708 ~ 3.0720)	ø78.12 (ø3.0755)

NOTE: Be sure to measure A-A, B-B and a, b and c

Chapter 2 Basic Engine
2. Cylinder Liners

4JH Series

2-3 Measuring cylinder liner projection

Make sure the cylinder liner flange projects only slightly above the block.

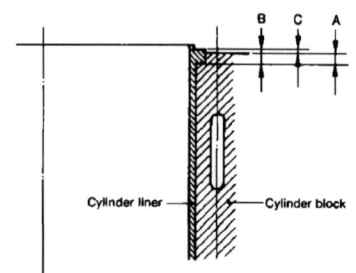

mm (in.)

A	3.46 ~ 3.50 (0.1362 ~ 0.1378)
B	3.53 ~ 3.55 (0.1390 ~ 0.1398)
C	0.03 ~ 0.09 (0.0011 ~ 0.0035)

NOTE: Excessive cylinder liner projection is frequently caused by incomplete removal of the rust on the ledge (Part D of figure) of the cylinder block.

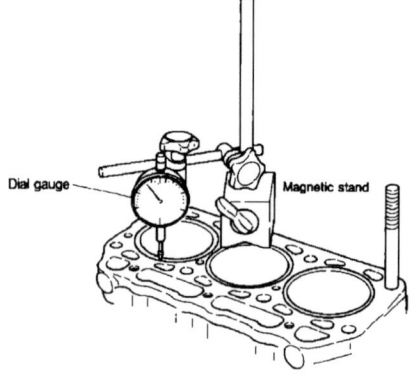

3. Cylinder Head

The cylinder head is of 4-cylinder integral construction, mounted with 18 bolts. Special alloy stellite with superior resistance to heat and wear is fitted on the seats, and the area between the valves is cooled by a water jet.

IMPORTANT:
Cylinder head assembly differs among engine models. If an incorrect cylinder head is installed, combustion performance will drop. Be sure to check the applicable engine model identification mark (I. D. Mark) on the cylinder head assembly to insure use of the correct part.

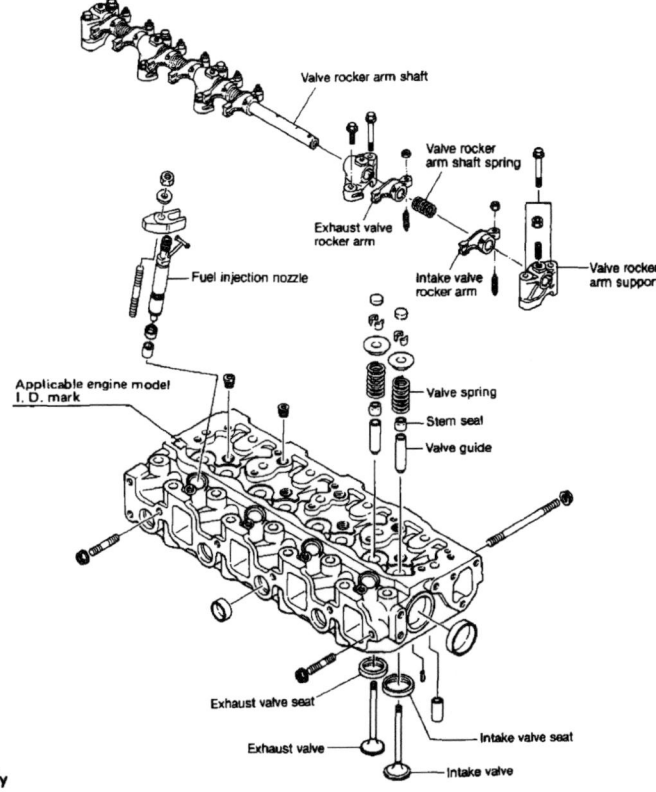

Cylinder Head Ass'y

	I.D. Mark	Applicable Engine Model & E/#	
Old type	1	4JHE	E/#01000 and before
	1	4JH-TE	E/#11000 and before
	5	4JH-HTE	E/#21000 and before
New type	SL	4JHE	E/#01001 and after
	SG	4JH-TE	E/#11001 and after
	SG	4JH-HTE	E/#21001 and after
	SG	4JH-DTE	E/#30101 and after

*Engines produced at YANMAR plant on and after June 21, 1985

Chapter 2 Basic Engine
3. Cylinder Head

4JHE·4JH-TE

3-1 Inspecting the cylinder head
The cylinder head is subjected to very severe operating conditions with repeated high pressure, high temperature and cooling. Thoroughly remove all the carbon and dirt after disassembly and carefully inspect all parts.

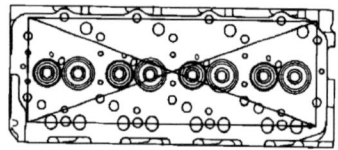

3-1.1 Distortion of the combustion surface
Carefully check for cylinder head distortion as this leads to gasket damage and compression leaks.
(1) Clean the cylinder head surface.
(2) Place a straight-edge along each of the four sides and each diagonal. Measure the clearance between the straight-edge and combustion surface with a feeler gauge.

Measurement procedure

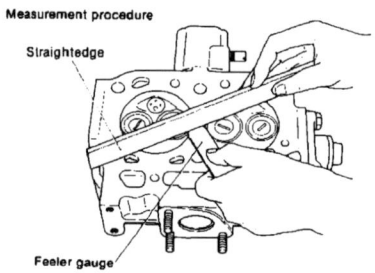

mm (in.)

	Standard	Wear limit
Cylinder head distortion	0.05 (0.0019) or less	0.15 (0.0059)

3-1.2 Checking for cracks in the combustion surface
Remove the fuel injection nozzle, intake and exhaust valve and clean the combustion surface. Check for discoloration or distortion and conduct a color check test to check for any cracks.

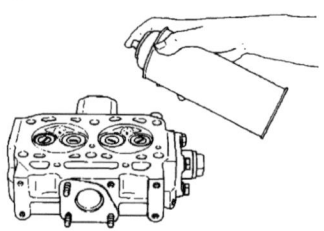

3-1.3 Checking the intake and exhaust valve seats
Check the surface and width of the valve seats.
If they are too wide, or if the surfaces are rough, correct to the following standards:

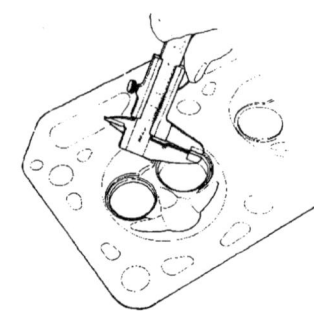

Seat angle	Intake	120°
	Exhaust	90°

mm (in.)

Seat width	Standard	Wear limit
Intake	1.28 (0.0504)	1.78 (0.0700)
Exhaust	1.77 (0.0697)	2.27 (0.0894)

Intake valve seat

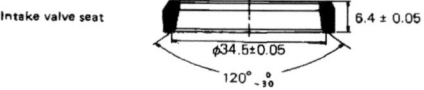

Exhaust valve seat

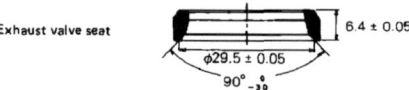

Standard dimension

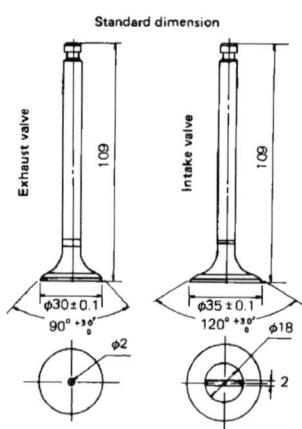

3-2 Valve seat correction procedure

The most common method for correcting unevenness of the seat surface with a seat grinder is as follows:
(1) Use a seat grinder to make the surface even.
   As the valve seat width will be enlarged, first use a 70° grinder, then grind the seat to the standard dimension with a 15° grinder.

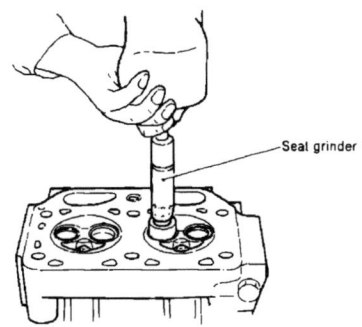
Seal grinder

Seat grinder	Intake valve	30°
	Exhaust valve	45°

NOTE: When seat adjustment is necessary, be sure to check the valve and valve guide. If the clearance exceeds the tolerance, replace the valve or the valve guide, and then grind the seat.

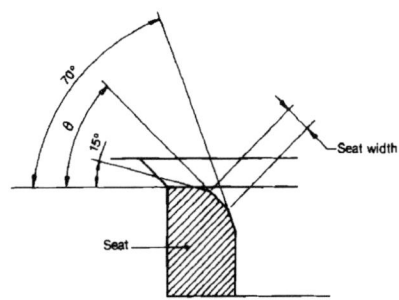
Seat width
Seat

(2) Knead valve compound with oil and finish the valve seat with a lapping tool.
(3) Final finishing should be done with oil only.

Lapping tool
Use a rubber cap type lapping tool for cylinders without a lapping tool groove slit.

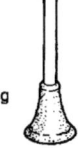

NOTE: Clean the valve and cylinder head with light oil or the equivalent after valve seat finishing is completed, and make sure that there are no grindings remaining.

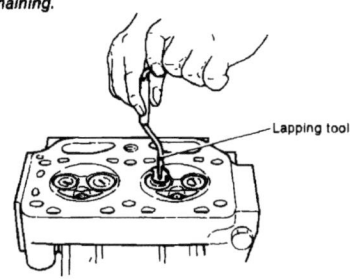
Lapping tool

NOTE: 1. Insert adjusting shims between the valve spring and cylinder head when seats have been refinished with a seat grinder.
2. Measure valve distortion after valve seat refinishing has been completed, and replace the valve and valve seat if it exceeds the tolerance.

3-3 Intake/exhaust valves, valve guides

3-3.1 Wearing and corrosion of valve stem

Replace the valve if the valve stem is excessively worn or corroded.

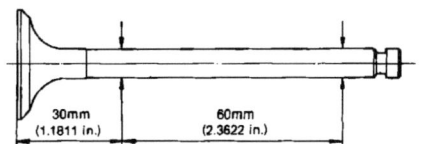
30mm (1.1811 in.)   60mm (2.3622 in.)

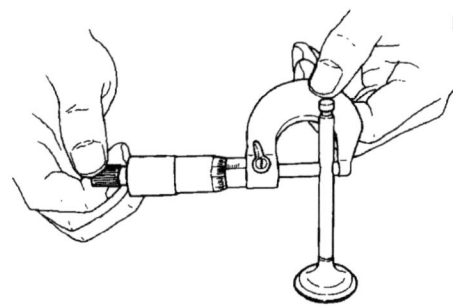

mm (in.)

Valve stem outside dia.	Standard	Wear limit
Intake	⌀7.960 ~ 7.975 (⌀0.3134 ~ 0.3140)	−0.13 (−0.0051)
Exhaust	⌀7.955 ~ 7.970 (⌀0.3132 ~ 0.3138)	−0.13 (−0.0051)

3-3.2 Inspection of valve seat wear and contact surface

Inspect for valve seat scratches and excessive wear. Check to make sure the contact surface is normal. The seat angle must be checked and adjusted if the valve seat contact surface is much smaller than the width of the valve seat.

NOTE: Keep in mind the fact that the intake and discharge valve have different diameters.

3-3.3 Valve sinking

Over long periods of use and repeated lappings, combustion efficiency may drop. Measure the sinking distance and replace the valve and valve seat if the valve sink exceeds the tolerance.

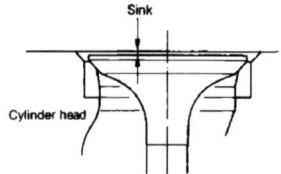

(2) Replacing the valve guide
Use the insertion tool and tap in the guide with a mallet.

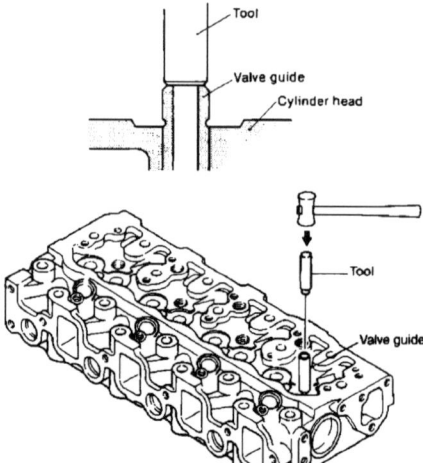

The intake valve guide and exhaust valve guide are of different shapes/dimensions. The one with a groove around it is the exhaust valve guide and the one without is the intake valve guide.

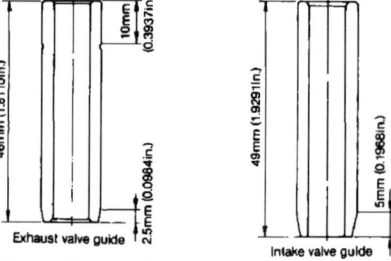

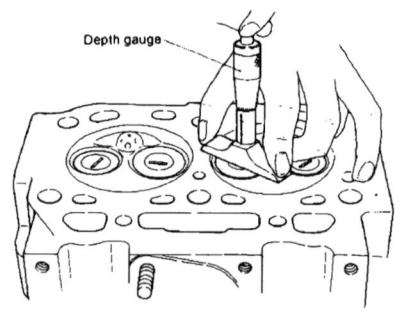

mm (in.)

	Standard	Wear limit
Valve sink	0.4 ~ 0.6 (0.0157 ~ 0.0236)	1.5 (0.0590)

3-3.4 Valve guide

(1) Measuring inner diameter of valve guide.
Measure the inner diameter of the valve guide and replace it if it exceeds the wear limit.

mm (in.)

		Standard	Wear limit
Valve guide inside dia.	Intake	ø8.015 ~ 8.030 (ø0.3156 ~ 0.3161)	+0.2 (0.0079)
	Exhaust	ø8.015 ~ 8.030 (ø0.3156 ~ 0.3161)	+0.2 (0.0079)

NOTE: The inner diameter standard dimensions assume a pressure fit.

(3) Valve guide projection
The valve guide should project 15mm from the top of the cylinder head.

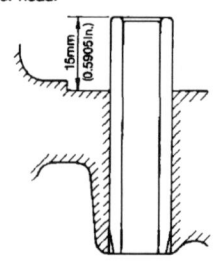

Chapter 2 Basic Engine
3. Cylinder Head

4JH Series

(4) Valve stem seals
The valve stem seals in the intake/exhaust valve guides cannot be re-used once they are removed—be sure to replace them.
When assembling the intake/exhaust valves, apply an adequate quantity of engine oil on the valve stem before inserting them.

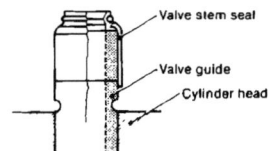

3-4 Valve springs
3-4.1 Checking valve springs
(1) Check the spring for scratches or corrosion.
(2) Measure the free length of the spring.

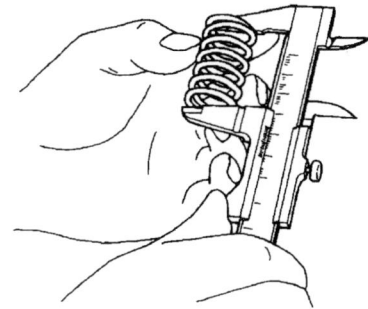

(3) Measure inclination.

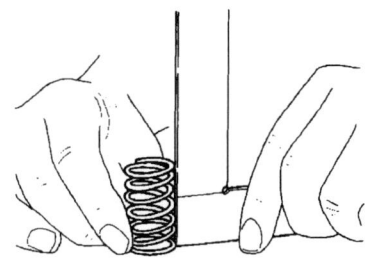

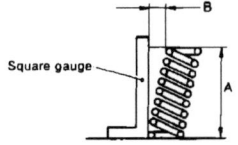

(4) Measure spring tension.

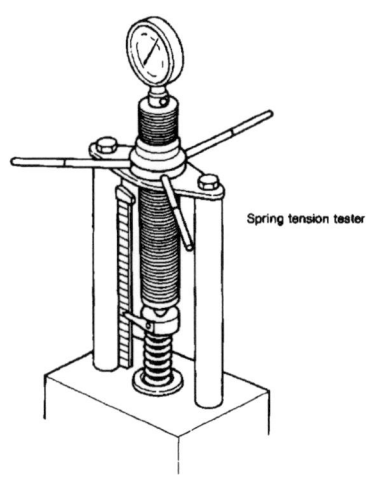

Spring tension tester

mm (in.)

Valve spring	Standard	Wear limit
Free length	44.4 (1.7480)	43 (1.6929)
Length when attached	40 (1.5748)	—
Load when attached	12kg (26.46 lb.)	10kg (22.05 lb.)

Assembling valve springs
The side with the smaller pitch (painted yellow) should face down (cylinder head).

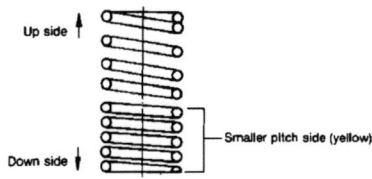

NOTE: *The pitch of the valve spring is not even. The side with the smaller pitch (yellow) should face down (cylinder head) when assembled.*

(5) Spring retainer and spring cotter
Inspect the inside face of the spring retainer, the outside surface of the spring cotter, the contact area of the spring cotter inside surface and the notch in the head of the valve stem. Replace the spring retainer and spring cotter when the contact area is less than 70%, or when the spring cotter has been recessed because of wear.

3-5 Assembling the cylinder head

Partially tighten the bolts in the specified order and then tighten to the specified torque, being careful that head does not get distorted.
(1) Clean out the cylinder head bolt holes.
(2) Check for foreign matter on the cylinder head surface that comes in contact with the block.
(3) Coat the head bolt threads and nut seats with lube oil.
(4) Use the positioning pins to line up the head gasket with the cylinder block.
(5) Match up the cylinder head with the head gasket and mount.

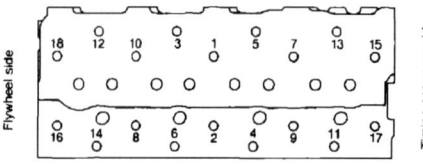

	kg·m (ft-lb)	
	First	Second
Tightening torque	3.5 ~ 4.5 (25.32 ~ 32.55)	7.5 ~ 8.5 (54.25 ~ 61.48)

3-6 Measuring top clearance

(1) Place a high quality fuse (Ø1.5mm (0.0591in.), 10mm (0.3937in.) long) in three positions on the flat part of the piston head.
(2) Assemble the cylinder head gasket and the cylinder block and tighten the bolts in the specified order to the specified torque.
(3) Turn the crank, (in the direction of engine revolution), and press the fuse against the piston until it breaks.
(4) Remove the head and take out the broken fuse.
(5) Measure the three positions where each fuse is broken and calculate the average.
(0.71 ~ 0.75mm (0.0280 ~ 0.0295in.) is ideal)

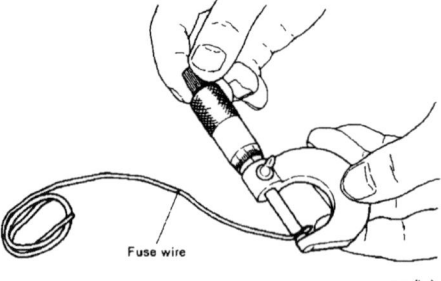

	mm (in.)
Top clearance	0.71 ~ 0.89 (0.0280 ~ 0.0350)

3-7 Intake and exhaust valve arms

Valve arm and valve arm bushing wear may change opening/closing timing of the valve, and may in turn affect engine performance according to the extent of the change.

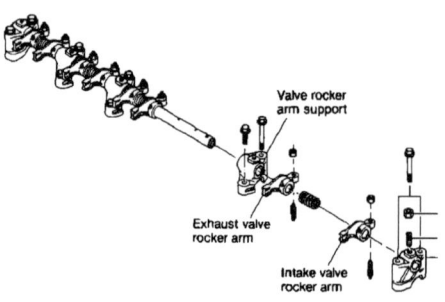

(1) Valve arm shaft and valve arm bushing
Measure the outer diameter of the shaft and the inner diameter of the bearing, and replace if wear exceeds the limit.

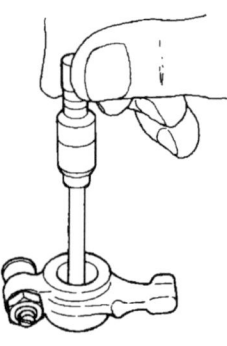

			mm (in.)
		Standard	Wear limit
Intake and exhaust valve rocker arm shaft outside dia.	A	15.966 ~ 15.984 (0.6285 ~ 0.6292)	15.955 (0.6281)
Intake and exhaust valve rocker arm bushing inside dia. (assembled)	B	16.000 ~ 16.018 (0.6299 ~ 0.6306)	16.090 (0.6334)
Valve rocker arm shaft and bushing clearance at assembly		0.016 ~ 0.052 (0.0006 ~ 0.0020)	0.135 (0.0053)

Replace the valve arm shaft bushing if it moves and replace the entire valve arm if there is no tightening clearance.

Chapter 2 Basic Engine
3. Cylinder Head

4JH Series

(2) Valve arm spring
Check the valve arm spring and replace it if it is corroded or worn.

(3) Valve arm and valve top retainer wear
Inspect the contact surface of the valve arm and replace it if there is abnormal wear or flaking.

(4) Inspect the contact surface of the valve clearance adjustment screw and push rod and replace if there is abnormal wear or flaking.

3-8 Adjustment of valve head clearance

(1) Make adjustments when the engine is cool.

	mm (in.)
Intake and exhaust head clearance	0.2 (0.0079)

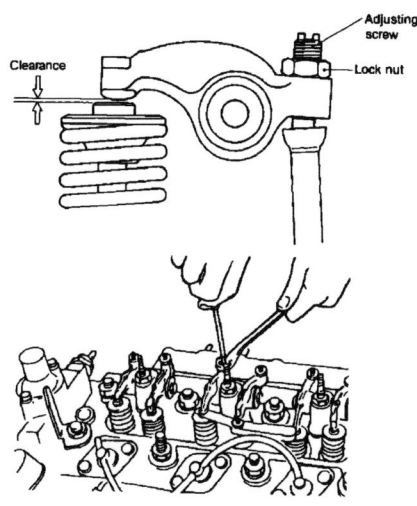

(2) Be sure that the opening and closing angles for both the intake and the exhaust valves are checked when the timing gear is disassembled (The gauge on the flywheel is read when the push rod turns the flywheel).

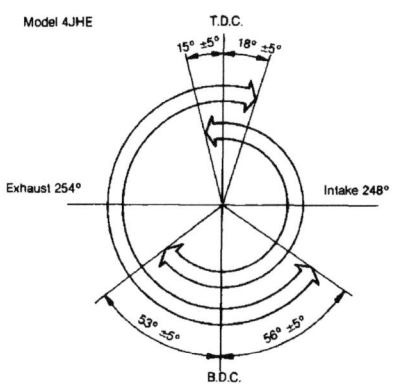

Model 4JHE

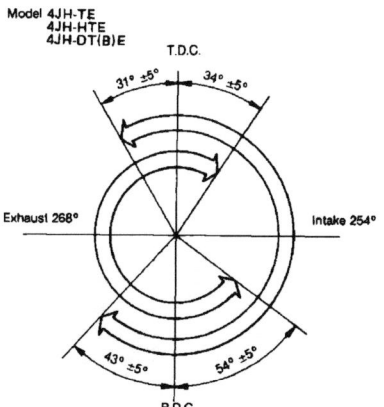

Model 4JH-TE
4JH-HTE
4JH-DT(B)E

	4JHE	4JH-TE 4JH-HTE 4JH-DT(B)E
Intake valve open	b.TDC	10° ~ 20°	26° ~ 36°
Intake valve closed	a.BDC	48° ~ 58°	38° ~ 48°
Exhaust valve open	b.BDC	51° ~ 61°	49° ~ 59°
Exhaust valve closed	a.TDC	13° ~ 23°	29° ~ 39°

4. Pistons and Piston Pins

Pistons are made of a special light alloy with superior thermal expansion characteristics, and the top of the piston forms a swirl type toroidal combustion chamber. The opposite face of the piston combustion surface is oil-jet cooled.
Pistons for engines with superchargers have a valve recess for the intake and exhaust valves.
The clearance between the piston and cylinder liner is kept at the proper value by the piston and cylinder liner property fit effected during assembly at the Yanmar factory.

IMPORTANT:
Piston shape differs among engine models. If an incorrect piston is installed, combustion performance will drop. Be sure to check the applicable engine model identification mark (I. D. Mark) on the piston to insure use of the correct part.

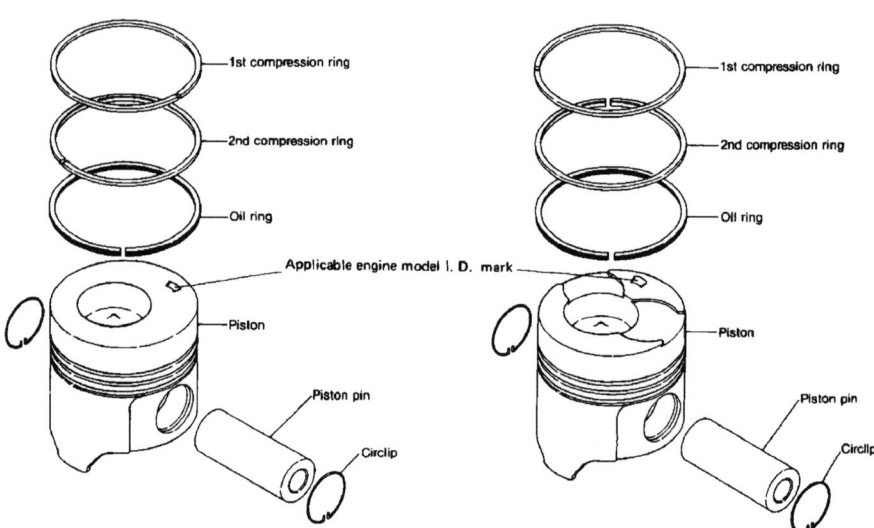

I. D. Mark for Piston

	I.D. Mark	Applicable Engine Model & E/#	
	1	4JHE	E/#01000 and before
Old type	2	4JH-TE	E/#11000 and before
	5	4JH-HTE	E/#21000 and before
	A	4JHE	E/#01001 and after
New type	B	4JH-TE	E/#11001 and after
	C	4JH-HTE	E/#21001 and after
	C	4JH-DTE	E/#30101 and after

*Engines produced at YANMAR plant on and after June 21, 1985

Chapter 2 Basic Engine
4. Piston and Piston Pins

4JH Series

4-1 Piston

4-1.1 Piston head and combustion surface

Remove the carbon that has accumulated on the piston head and combustion surface, taking care not to scratch the piston. Check the combustion surface for any damage.

4-1.2 Measurement of piston outside diameter/inspection

(1) Replace the piston if the outsides of the piston or ring grooves are worn.
(2) Measure the piston 22mm (0.8661in.) from the bottom at right angles to the piston pin.

4-1.3 Replacing the piston

A floating type piston pin is used in this engine. The piston pin can be pressed into the piston pin hole at room temperature (coat with oil to make it slide in easily).

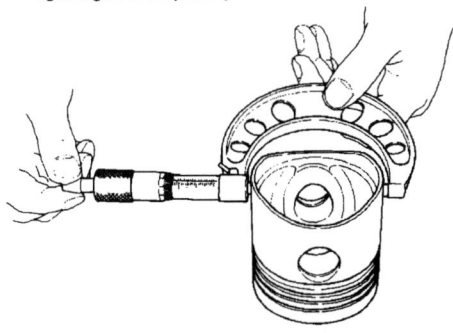

4-2 Piston pin

Measure the outer diameter and replace the pin If it is excessively worn.

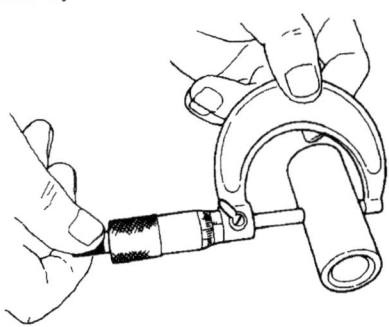

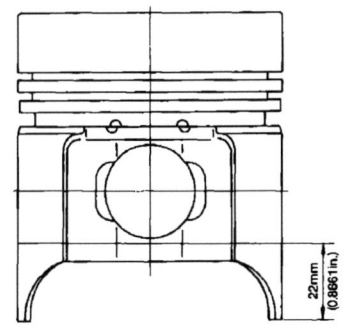

	mm (in.)
Standard	Wear limit
77.91 ~ 77.94 (3.0673 ~ 3.0685)	77.81 (3.0633)

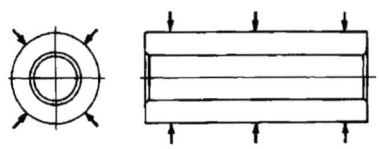

mm (in.)

	Standard	Wear limit
Piston pin insert hole dia.	ø26.000 ~ 26.009 (ø1.0236 ~ 1.0240)	+0.020 (0.0008)
Piston pin outside dia.	ø25.987 ~ 26.000 (ø1.0231 ~ 1.0236)	−0.025 (0.0009)
Standard clearance	0 ~ 0.022 (0 ~ 0.0009)	0.045 (0.0018)

4-3 Piston rings

There are 2 compression rings and 1 oil ring. The absence of an oil ring on the piston skirt prevents oil from being kept on the thrust surface and in turn provides good lubrication.

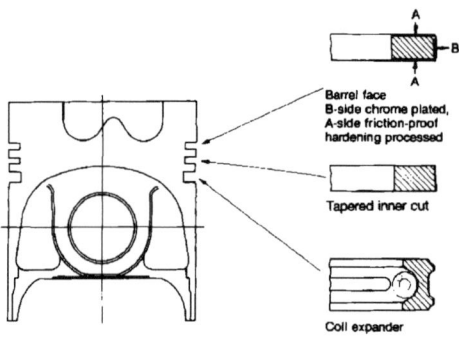

Barrel face
B-side chrome plated,
A-side friction-proof hardening processed

Tapered inner cut

Coil expander

		Standard	Wear limit
First piston ring	Groove width	2.060 ~ 2.075 (0.0811 ~ 0.0816)	—
	Ring width	1.975 ~ 1.990 (0.0777 ~ 0.0783)	—
	Groove and ring clearance	0.070 ~ 0.100 (0.0027 ~ 0.0039)	0.2 (0.0078)
Second piston ring	Groove width	2.025 ~ 2.040 (0.0797 ~ 0.0803)	—
	Ring width	1.975 ~ 1.990 (0.0777 ~ 0.0783)	—
	Groove and ring clearance	0.035 ~ 0.065 (0.0013 ~ 0.0025)	0.2 (0.0078)
Oil ring	Groove width	4.020 ~ 4.035 (0.1582 ~ 0.1588)	—
	Ring width	3.975 ~ 3.990 (0.1564 ~ 0.1570)	—
	Groove and ring clearance	0.030 ~ 0.060 (0.0011 ~ 0.0023)	0.2 (0.0078)

mm (in.)

4-3.2 Measuring piston ring gap

Press the piston ring onto a piston liner and measure the piston ring gap with a gauge. Press on the ring about 30mm (1.811in.) from the bottom of the liner.

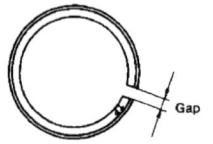
Gap

4-3.1 Measuring the rings

Measure the thickness and width of the rings, and the ring-to-groove clearance after installation. Replace if wear exceeds the limit.

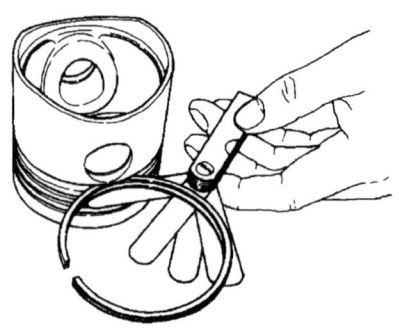

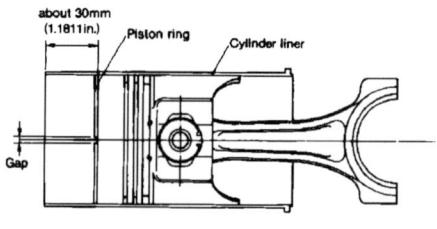

about 30mm (1.1811in.) Piston ring Cylinder liner

Gap

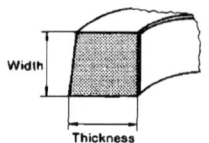

Width

Thickness

	Standard	Wear limit
First piston ring gap	0.25 ~ 0.40 (0.0098 ~ 0.0157)	1.5 (0.0590)
Second piston ring gap	0.25 ~ 0.40 (0.0098 ~ 0.0157)	1.5 (0.0590)
Oil ring gap	0.20 ~ 0.40 (0.0078 ~ 0.0157)	1.5 (0.0590)

mm (in.)

Chapter 2 Basic Engine
4. Piston and Piston Pins
_____ 4JH Series

4-3.3 Replacing the piston rings

(1) Thoroughly clean the ring grooves when replacing piston rings.
(2) The side with the manufacturer's mark (near piston ring gap) should face up.

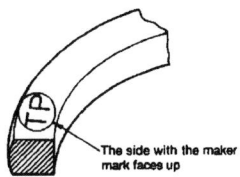
The side with the maker mark faces up

(3) After fitting the piston ring, make sure it moves easily and smoothly.
(4) Stagger the piston rings at 120° intervals, making sure none of them line up with the piston.

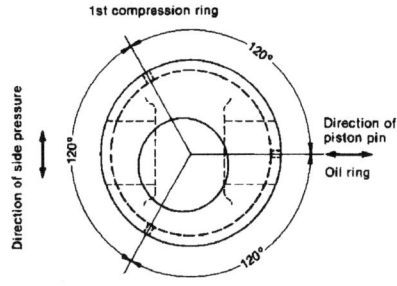
1st compression ring
Direction of piston pin
Oil ring
Direction of side pressure
2nd compression ring

(5) The oil ring is provided with a coil expander. The coil expander joint should be opposite (staggered 180°) the oil ring gap.

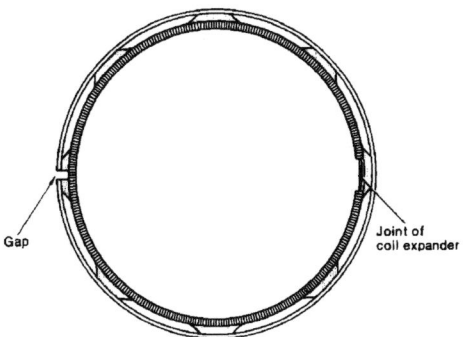
Gap
Joint of coil expander

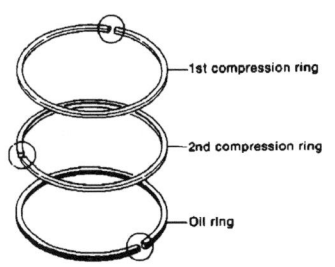
1st compression ring
2nd compression ring
Oil ring

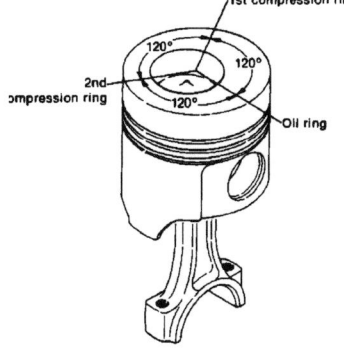
1st compression ring
2nd compression ring
Oil ring

2-16

Printed in Japan
0000A0A1647

5. Connecting Rod

The connecting rod is made of high-strength forged carbon steel.
The large end with the 3-layer kelmet can be separated into two and the small end has a 2-layer copper alloy coil bushing.

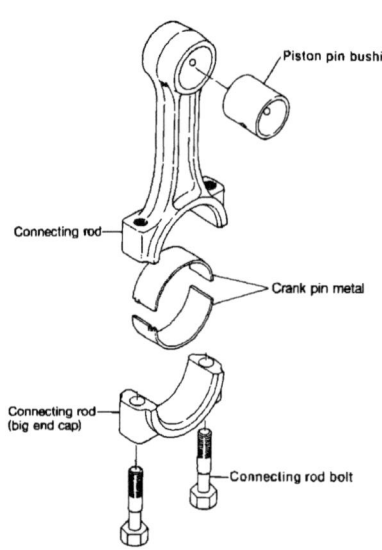

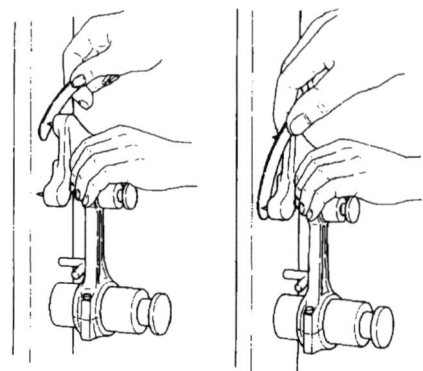

Measuring twist and parallelity

	Standard	Wear limit
Connecting rod twist and parallelity	0.05 (0.0019)	0.07 (0.0027)

mm (in.)

5-1.2 Checking thrust clearance

Fit the respective crank pins to the connecting rod and check to make sure that the clearance in the crankshaft direction is correct.

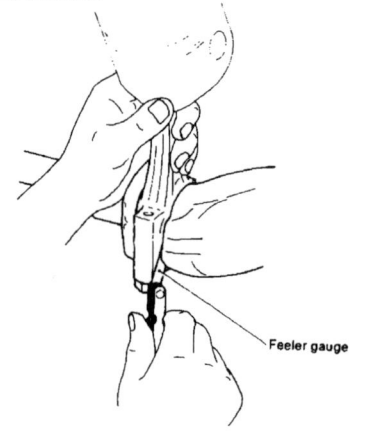

5-1 Inspecting the connection rod

5-1.1 Twist and parallelism of the large and small ends

Insert the measuring tool into the large and small ends of the connecting rod. Measure the extent of twist and parallelism and replace if they exceed the tolerance.

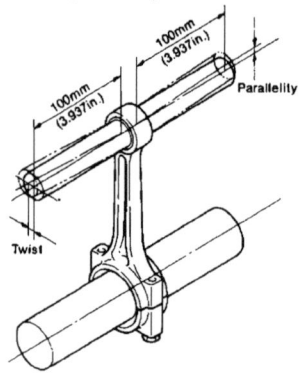

mm (in.)

	Standard	Wear limit
Connecting rod side clearance	0.20 ~ 0.40 (0.0078 ~ 0.0157)	0.55 (0.0216)

Chapter 2 Basic Engine
5. Connecting Rod
4JH Series

5-2 Crank pin bushing

5-2.1 Checking crank pin bushing

Check for flaking, melting or seizure on the contact surface.

5-2.2 Measuring crank pin oil clearance

Use a plastic gauge.

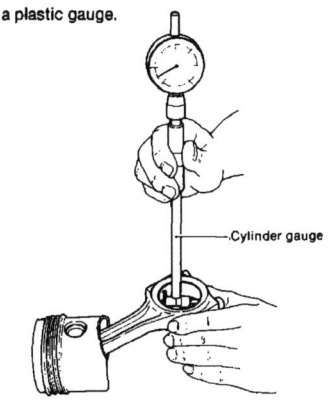

Procedure
(1) Use the press gauge (Plastigage) for measuring oil clearance in the crank pin.
(2) Mount the connecting rod on the crank pin (tighten to specified torque).

Connecting rod tightening torque	4.5 ~ 5.0 kg-m (32.5 ~ 36.1 ft-lb)

(3) Remove the connecting rod and measure the broken plastic gauge with measuring paper.

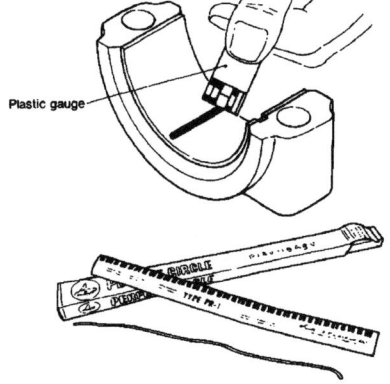

5-2.3 Precautions on replacement of crank pin bushing

(1) Wash the crank pin bushing.
(2) Wash the large end cap, mount the crank pin bushing and make sure that it fits tightly on the large end cap.
(3) When assembling the connecting rod, match up the large end and large end cap number. Coat the bolts with engine oil and gradually tighten them alternately to the specified torque.
If a torque wrench is not available, make match marks on the bolt heads and large end cap (to indicate the proper torque position) and retighten the bolts to those positions.

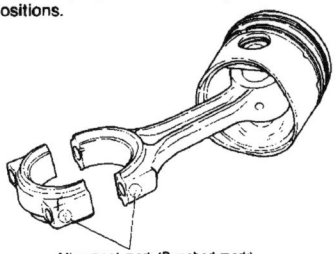

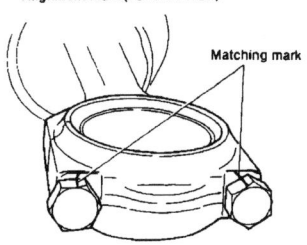

(4) Make sure there is no sand, metal cuttings or other foreign matter in the lube oil, and that the crankshaft is not scratched. Take special care in cleaning the oil holes.

5-3 Piston pin bushing

(1) Measuring piston pin clearance
Excessive piston pin bushing wear may result in damage to the piston pin or the piston itself.

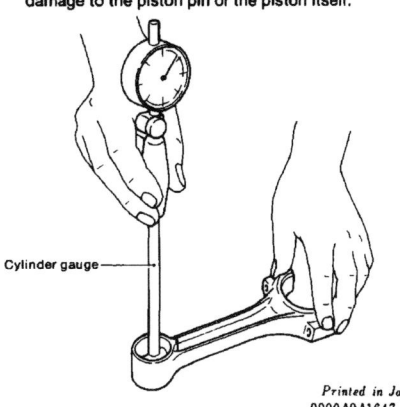

Chapter 2 Basic Engine
5. Connecting Rod

4JH Series

	Standard	Wear limit
	mm (in.)	
Piston pin bushing inside dia.	26.025 ~ 26.038 (1.0246 ~ 1.0251)	26.1 (1.0275)
Piston pin and bushing oil clearance	0.025 ~ 0.051 (0.0009 ~ 0.002)	0.11 (0.0043)

(2) Replacing piston pin bushing
1) When the bushing for the connecting rod piston pin is either worn out or damaged, replace it by using the "piston pin extracting tool" installed on a press.

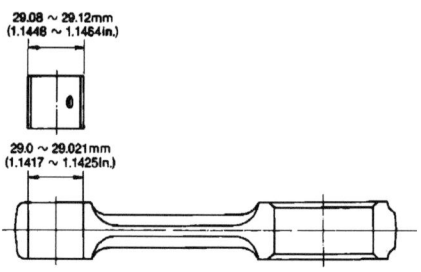

29.08 ~ 29.12mm
(1.1448 ~ 1.1464in.)

29.0 ~ 29.021mm
(1.1417 ~ 1.1425in.)

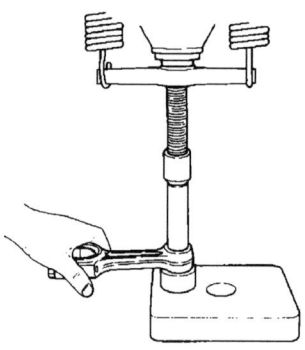

NOTE: Force the piston pin bushing into position so that its oil hole coincides with the hole on the small end of the connecting rod.

2) After forcing the piston pin bushing into position, finish the inner surface of the bushing by using a pin honing machine or reamer so that it fits the piston pin to be used.

5-4 Assembling piston and connecting rod
The piston and connecting rod should be assembled so that the match mark on the connecting rod large end faces the fuel injection pump side and the combustion chamber above the piston is close to the fuel injection pump.

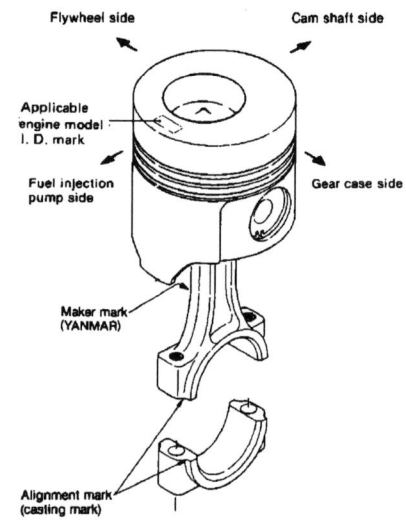

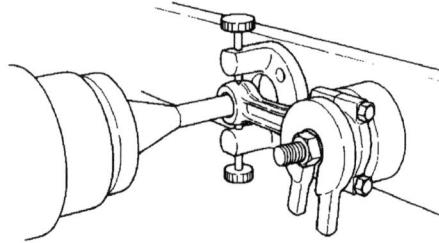

NOTE: Attach the bushing to the piston pin so that a pin, coated with engine oil can be pushed into position with your thumb.

I. D. Mark for Piston

	I.D. Mark	Applicable Engine Model & E/#
Old type	1	4JHE	E/#01000 and before
	2	4JH-TE	E/#11000 and before
	5	4JH-HTE	E/#21000 and before
New type	A	4JHE	E/#01001 and after
	B	4JH-TE	E/#11001 and after
	C	4JH-HTE	E/#21001 and after
	C	4JH-DTE	E/#30101 and after

*Engines produced at YANMAR plant on and after June 21, 1985

Printed in Japan
0000A0A1647

2-19

Chapter 2 Basic Engine
6. Crankshaft and Main Bearing — 4JH Series

6. Crankshaft and Main Bearing

The crank pin and crank journal have been induction hardened for superior durability, and the crankshaft is provided with four balance weights for optional balance. The crankshaft main bearing is of the hanger type. The upper metal (cylinder block side) is provided with an oil groove. There is no oil groove on the lower metal (bearing cap side). The bearing cap (location cap) of the flywheel side has a thrust metal which supports the thrust load.

IMPORTANT:
Although the size is identical, the crankshaft material of models 4JHE and 4JH-TE differ from that used in models 4JH-HTE and 4JH-DTE.
Please note that the crankshaft for models 4JHE and 4JH-TE cannot be used for models 4JH-HTE and 4JH-DTE since the crankshaft is not durable enough.

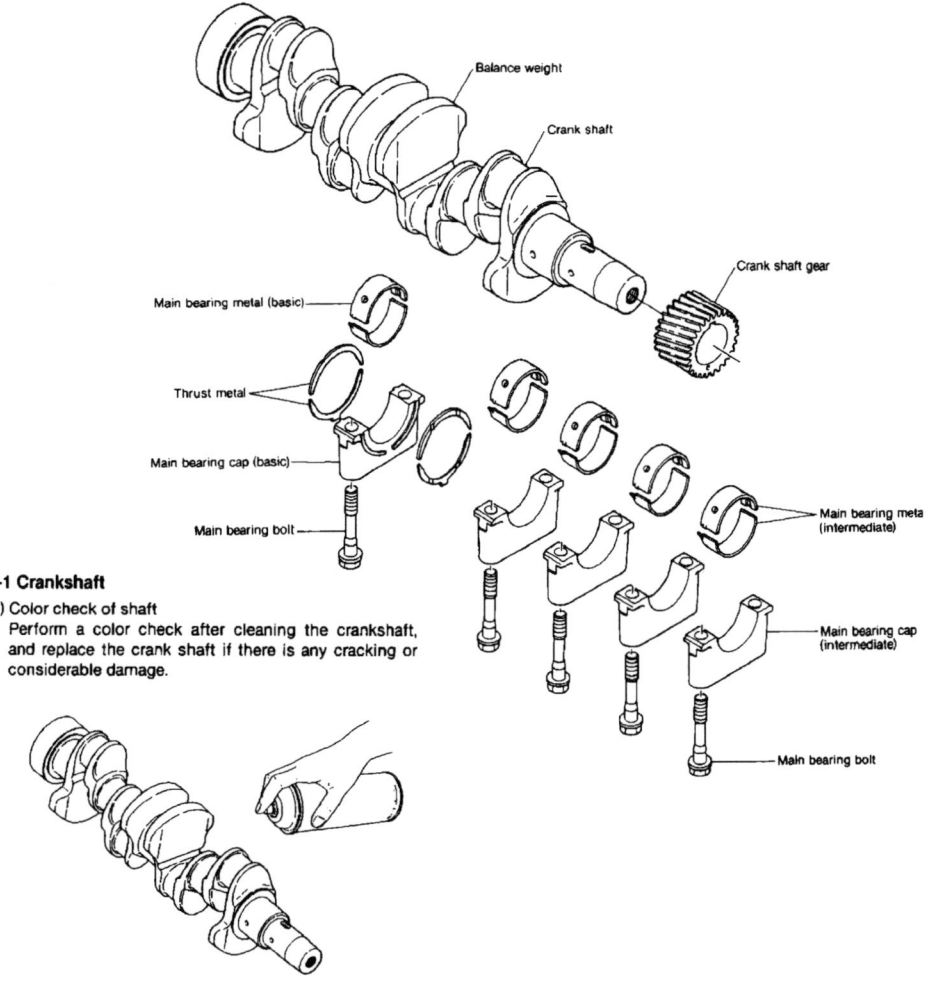

6-1 Crankshaft

(1) Color check of shaft
Perform a color check after cleaning the crankshaft, and replace the crank shaft if there is any cracking or considerable damage.

Chapter 2 Basic Engine
6. Crankshaft and Main Bearing

4JH Series

(2) Bending of the crankshaft
Support the crankshaft with V-blocks at both ends of the journals. Measure the deflection of the center journal with a dial gauge while rotating the crankshaft to check the extent of crankshaft bending.

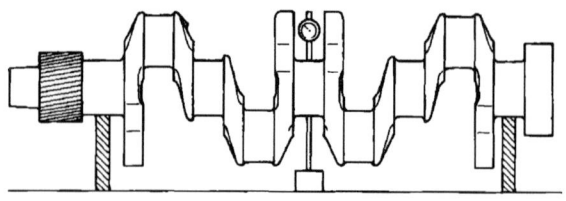
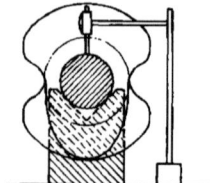

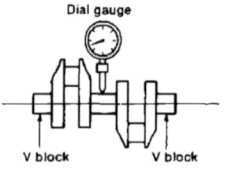
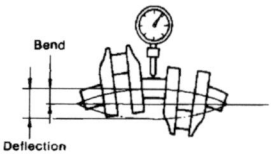

Crankshaft bend	Less than 0.02mm (0.0007 in.)

(3) Measuring the crank pin and journal
Measure the extent of journal wear (roundness, taper). Regrind it to the proper shape if it is within the outer diameter limit, and replace if not.

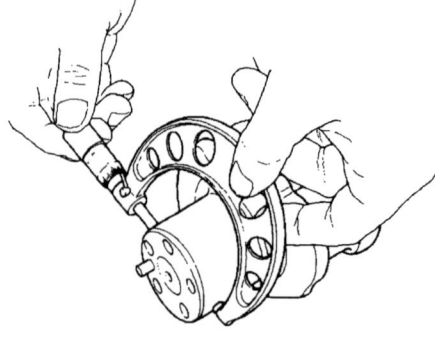
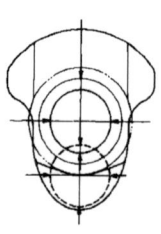
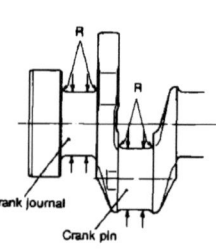

mm (in.)

		Standard	Wear limit
Crank pin	Outside dia.	47.952 ~ 47.962 (1.8878 ~ 1.8882)	47.75 (1.8799)
	Bushing inside dia.	48.000 ~ 48.045 (1.8897 ~ 1.8915)	48.10 (1.8937)
	Crank pin and bushing oil clearance	0.038 ~ 0.093 (0.0014 ~ 0.0036)	0.25 (0.0098)
Crank journal	Outside dia.	49.952 ~ 49.962 (1.9666 ~ 1.9670)	49.75 (1.9586)
	Bushing inside dia.	50.000 ~ 50.045 (1.9685 ~ 1.9702)	50.10 (1.9724)
	Crank journal and bushing oil clearance	0.038 ~ 0.093 (0.0014 ~ 0.0036)	0.25 (0.0098)
Fillet rounding of crank pin and journal		3.500 ~ 3.800 (0.1377 ~ 0.1496)	

Chapter 2 Basic Engine
6. Crankshaft and Main Bearing

4JH Series

(4) Checking side clearance of the crankshaft
After assembling the crankshaft, tighten the main bearing cap to the specified torque, and move the crankshaft to one side, placing a dial gauge on one end of the shaft to measure thrust clearance.
This measurement can also be effected by inserting the gauge directly into the clearance between the thrust bearing and crankshaft thrust surface.
Replace the thrust bearing if it is worn beyond the limit.

mm (in.)

	Standard	Wear limit
Crankshaft side gap	0.090 ~ 0.271 (0.0035 ~ 0.0106)	0.30 (0.0118)

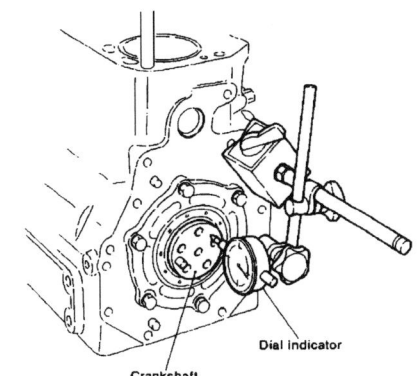

Dial indicator
Crankshaft

6-2 Main bearing

(1) Inspecting the main bearing
Check for flaking, seizure or burning of the contact surface and replace if necessary.
(2) Measuring the inner diameter of metal
Tighten the cap to the specified torque and measure the inner diameter of the metal.

Bearing cap bolt tightening torque	9.5 ~ 10.5 kg·m (68.71 ~ 75.84 ft-lb)

NOTE: When assembling the bearing cap, keep the following in mind.
1) The lower metal (cap side) has no oil groove.
2) The upper metal (cylinder block side) has an oil groove.
3) Check the cylinder block alignment No.
4) The "FW" on the cap lies on the flywheel side.

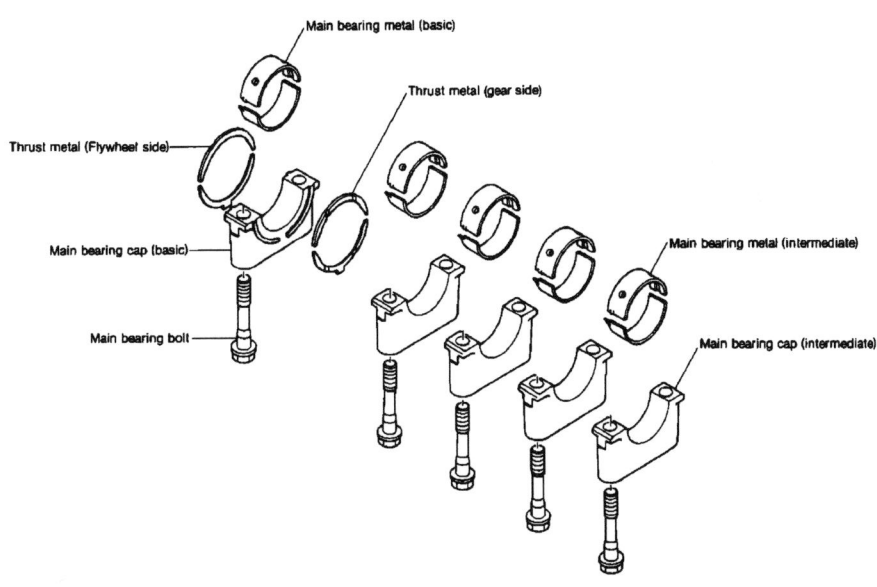

2-22

Printed in Japan
0000A0A1647

7. Camshaft and Tappets

7-1 Camshaft

The camshaft is normalized and the cam and bearing surfaces are surface hardened and ground. The cams have a curve that minimizes the repeated shock on the valve seats and maximizes valve seat life.

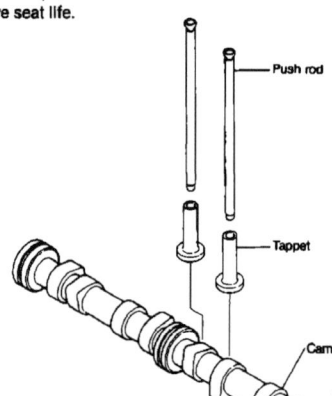

(1) Checking the camshaft side gap

The standard bearing near the end of the camshaft by the cam gear receives the load, resulting in rapid wear of the end of the bearing and enlargement of the side gap. Therefore, measure the thrust gap before disassembly. As the cam gear is shrink-fitted to the cam, be careful when replacing the thrust bearing.

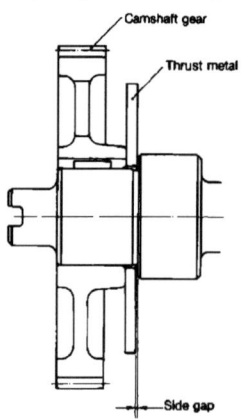

(2) Measure the camshaft height, and replace the cam if it is worn beyond the limit.

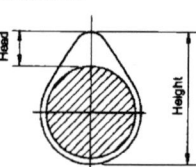

	Standard	Wear limit
Camshaft side gap	0.05 ~ 0.25 (0.0019 ~ 0.0098)	0.4 (0.0157)

Camshaft height   mm (in.)

Engine model		Standard	Wear limit
4JHE	Intake cam	38.66 ~ 38.74 (1.5220 ~ 1.5251)	38.4 (1.5118)
	Exhaust cam	38.66 ~ 38.74 (1.5220 ~ 1.5251)	38.4 (1.5118)
4JH-TE 4JH-HTE 4JH-DT(B)S	Intake cam	38.66 ~ 38.74 (1.5220 ~ 1.5251)	38.4 (1.5118)
	Exhaust cam	38.86 ~ 38.94 (1.5299 ~ 1.5330)	38.6 (1.5196)

Chapter 2 Basic Engine
7. Camshaft and Tappets — 4JH Series

(3) Measure the camshaft outer diameter and the camshaft bearing inner diameter. Replace if they exceed the wear limit or are damaged.

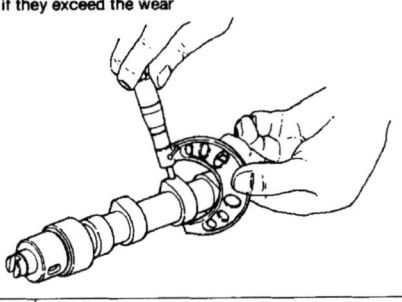

mm (in.)

	Gear case side	Standard Intermediate	Flywheel side	Wear limit
Camshaft journal outside dia.	44.925 ~ 44.950 (1.7687 ~ 1.7696)	44.910 ~ 44.935 (1.7681 ~ 1.7690)	44.925 ~ 44.950 (1.7687 ~ 1.7696)	44.8 (1.7637)
Camshaft journal bushing inside dia.	44.990 ~ 45.050 (1.7712 ~ 1.7736)	—	—	—
Cylinder block bearing inside dia.	—	45.000 ~ 45.025 (1.7716 ~ 1.7726)	45.000 ~ 45.025 (1.7716 ~ 1.7726)	—
Oil clearance	0.040 ~ 0.130 (0.0015 ~ 0.0050)	0.065 ~ 0.115 (0.0025 ~ 0.0045)	0.050 ~ 0.100 (0.0019 ~ 0.0039)	0.2 (0.0078)

(4) Bending of the crankshaft
Support both ends of the crankshaft with V-blocks, place a dial gauge against the central bearing areas and measure bending. Replace if excessive.

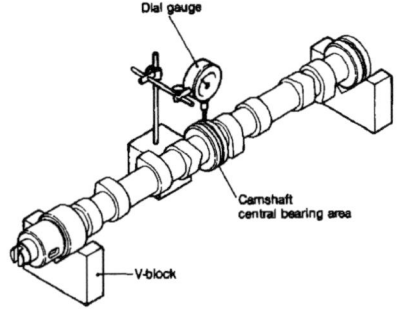

NOTE: The reading on the dial gauge is divided by two to obtain the extent of bending.

mm (in.)

	Wear limit
Camshaft deflection	0.02 (0.0007)

7-2 Tappets

(1) The tappets are offset to rotate during operation and thereby prevent uneven wearing. Check the contact of each tappet and replace if excessively or unevenly worn.

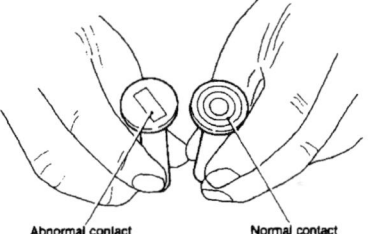

Abnormal contact — Normal contact

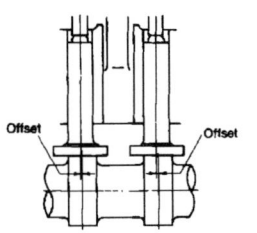

NOTE: When removing tappets, be sure to keep them separate for each cylinder and intake/exhaust valve.

Chapter 2 Basic Engine
7. Camshaft and Tappets

(2) Measure the outer diameter of the tappet, and replace if worn beyond the limit.

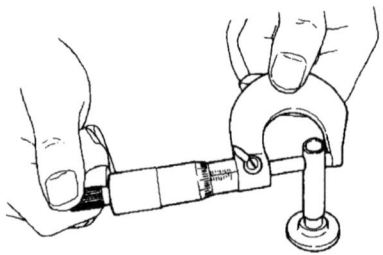

mm (in.)

	Standard	Wear limit
Tappet stem outside dia.	11.975 ~ 11.990 (0.4714 ~ 0.4720)	11.93 (0.4696)
Tappet guide hole inside dia. (cylinder block)	12.000 ~ 12.018 (0.4724 ~ 0.4731)	12.05 (0.4744)
Tappet stem and guide hole oil clearance	0.010 ~ 0.043 (0.0003 ~ 0.0016)	0.10 (0.0039)

(3) Measuring push rods.
Measure the length and bending of the push rods.

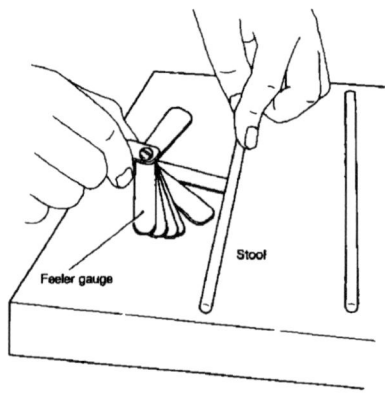

mm (in.)

	Standard	Wear limit
Push rod length	178.25 ~ 178.75 (7.0177 ~ 7.0374)	—
Push rod bend	Less than 0.03 (0.0011)	0.3 (0.0118)
Push rod dia.	8 (0.3149)	—

8. Timing Gear

The timing gear is helical type for minimum noise and specially treated for high durability.

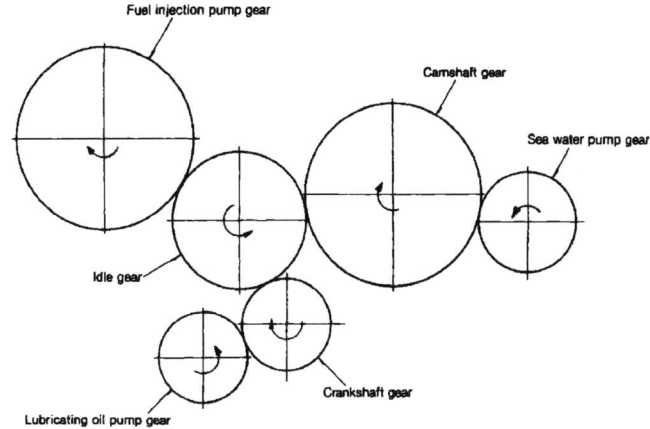

mm (in.)

	No. of teeth	Face width	Spiral angle	Center distance	Back lash	Back lash Wear limit
Sea water pump gear	31	12.0	right	92.544 ~ 92.592 (3.6434 ~ 3.6453)	0.04 ~ 0.12 (0.0015 ~ 0.0047)	0.2 (0.0078)
Camshaft gear	56	18.0	left	105.318 ~ 105.380 (4.1463 ~ 4.1488)	0.04 ~ 0.12 (0.0015 ~ 0.0047)	0.2 (0.0078)
Idle gear	43	18.0	right			
Crankshaft gear	28	40.0	left	75.525 ~ 75.573 (2.9734 ~ 2.9753)	0.04 ~ 0.12 (0.0015 ~ 0.0047)	0.2 (0.0078)
Lubricating oil pump gear	29	8.0	right	60.629 ~ 60.677 (2.3869 ~ 2.3888)	0.04 ~ 0.12 (0.0015 ~ 0.0047)	0.2 (0.0078)
Idle gear	43	18.0	right	105.254 ~ 105.316 (4.1438 ~ 4.1462)	0.04 ~ 0.12 (0.0015 ~ 0.0047)	0.2 (0.0078)
Fuel injection pump gear	56	10.0	left			

8-1 Inspecting the gears

(1) Inspect the gears and replace if the teeth are damaged or worn.
(2) Measure the backlash of all gears that mesh, and replace the meshing gears as a set if wear exceeds the limit.

NOTE: If backlash is excessive, it will not only result in excessive noise and gear damage, but also lead to bad valve and fuel injection timing and a decrease in engine performance.

(3) Idling gear
The bushing is pressure fitted into the idling gear. Measure the bushing inner diameter and the outer diameter of the shaft, and replace the bushing or idling gear shaft if the oil clearance exceeds the wear limit.
A, B and C are inscribed on the end of the idling gear. When assembling, these marks should align with those on the cylinder block.

Chapter 2 Basic Engine
8. Timing Gear

4JH Series

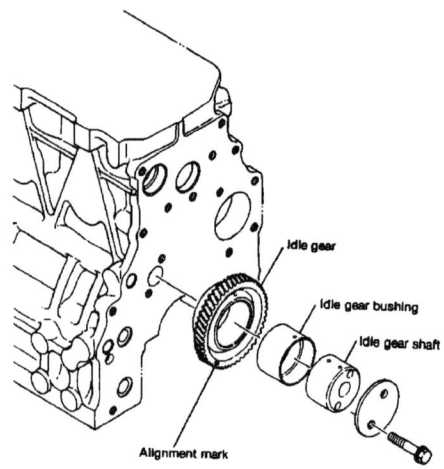

	Standard	mm (in.) Wear limit
Idle shaft dia.	45.950 ~ 45.975 (1.8090 ~ 1.8100)	45.88 (1.8062)
Idle shaft bushing inside dia.	46.000 ~ 46.025 (1.8110 ~ 1.8120)	—
Idle shaft and bushing oil clearance	0.025 ~ 0.075 (0.0009 ~ 0.0029)	0.15 (0.0059)

8-2 Gear timing marks

Match up the timing marks on each gear when assembling (A, B and C).

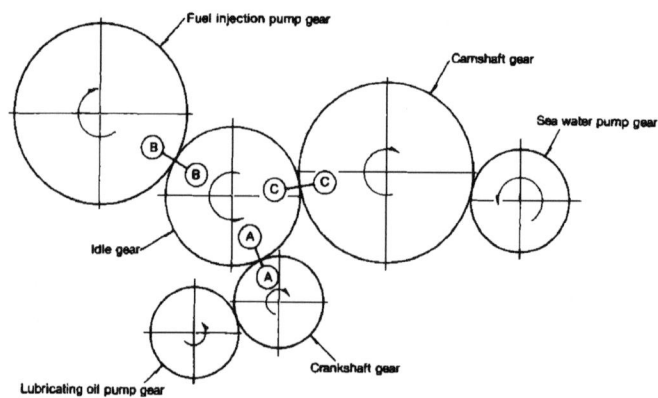

2-27

9. Flywheel and Housing

The function of the flywheel is, through inertia, to rotate the crankshaft in a uniform and smooth manner by absorbing the turning force created during the combustion stroke of the engine, and by compensating for the decrease in turning force during the other strokes.

The flywheel is mounted and secured by 6 bolts on the crankshaft end at the opposite end to the gear case; it is covered by the mounting flange (flywheel housing) which is bolted to the cylinder block.

On the crankshaft side of the flywheel is the fitting surface for the damper disc, through which the rotation of the crankshaft is transmitted to the input shaft of the reduction and reversing gear. The reduction and reversing gear is fitted to the mounting flange.

The flywheels unbalanced force on the shaft center must be kept below the specified value for the crankshaft as the flywheel rotates with the crankshaft at high speed. To achieve this, the balance is adjusted by drilling holes in the side of the flywheel, and the unbalanced momentum is adjusted by drilling holes in the circumference.

The ring gear is shirink fitted onto the circumference of the flywheel, and this ring gear serves to start the engine by meshing with the starter motor pinion.

The stamped letter and line which show top dead center of each cylinder are positioned on the flywheel circumference, and by matching these marks with the arrow mark at the hole of the flywheel housing, the rotary position of the crankshaft can be ascertained in order to adjust tappet clearance or fuel injection timing.

9-1 Specifications of flywheel

Outside dia. of flywheel		mm	Ø330
Width of flywheel		mm	47
Weight of flywheel (including ring gear)		kg	13.17
GD^2 value		kg-m²	1.10
Circumferential speed		m/s	62.2 (3600rpm)
Speed fluctuation rate		δ	1/346 (3600rpm)
Allowable amount of unbalance		g-cm	22
Fixing part of damper disc	Pitch circle dia. of bolts	mm	170
	No. of bolts × bolt dia.		6-M8 thread equally spaced
Fixing part of crankshaft	Pitch circle dia. of bolts	mm	66
	No. of thread holes	mm	6-M10
	Fit joint dia.		Ø85.000 ~ 85.035
Model of reduction and reversing gear			KBW-20 & KBW-21
Mounting flange No.			SAE No.4 (in metric unit)
Ring gear	Center dia.	mm	322.58
	No of teeth		127

Chapter 2 Basic Engine
9. Flywheel and Housing
4JH Series

9-2 Dimensions of flywheel and mounting flange

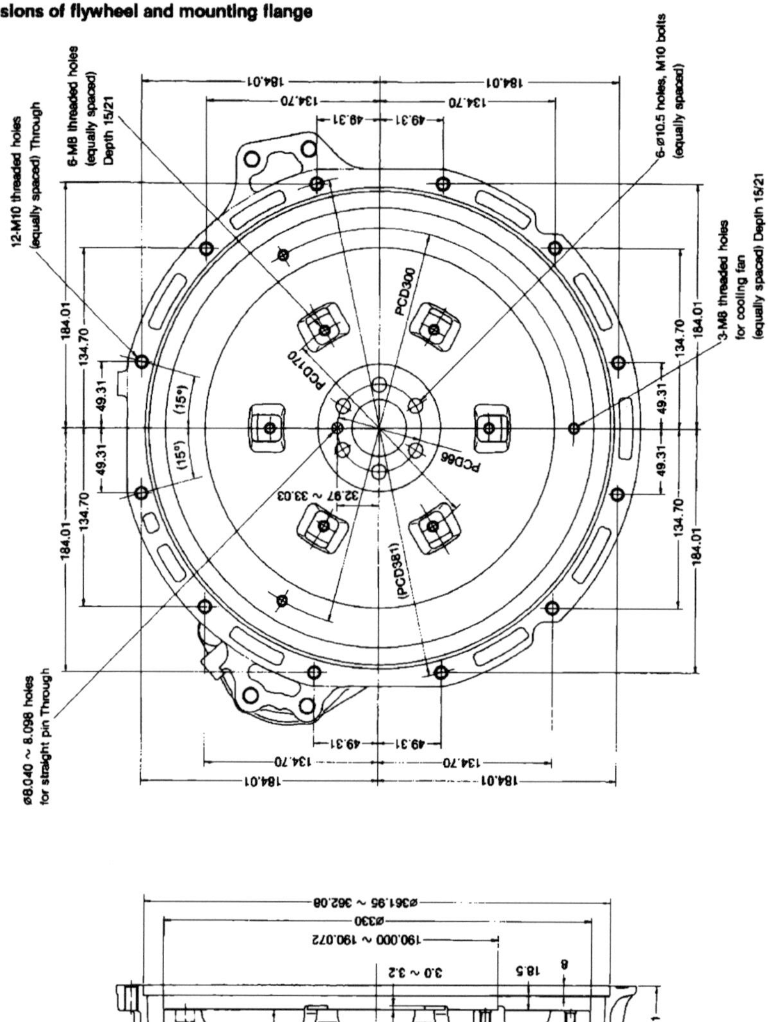

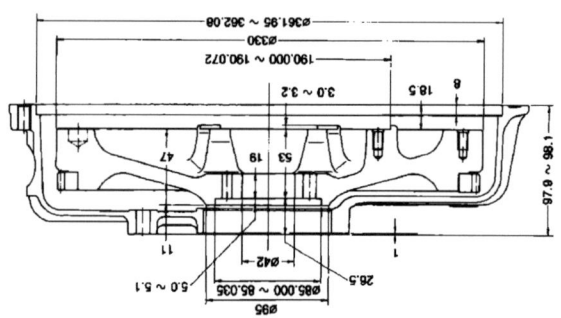

Chapter 2 Basic Engine
9. Flywheel and Housing

4JH Series

9-3 Ring gear
When replacing the ring gear due to excessive wear or damaged teeth, heat the ring gear evenly at its circumference, and after it has expanded drive it gradually off the flywheel by tapping it with a hammer, a copper bar or something similar around the whole circumference.

	mm (in.)
Interference of ring gear	0.158 ~ 0.250 (0.0062 ~ 0.0098)

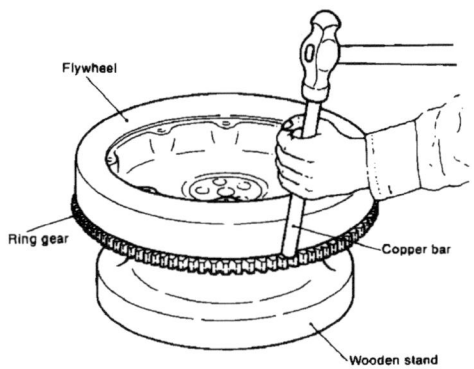

9-4 Position of top dead center and fuel injection timing
(1) Marking

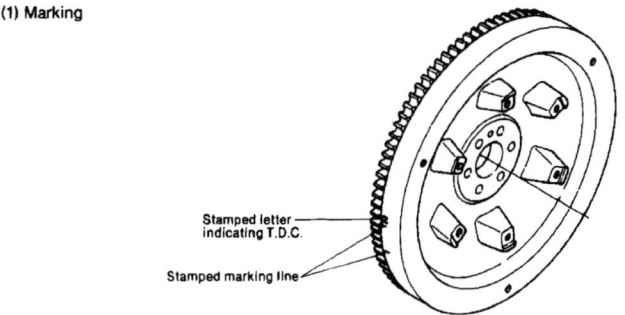

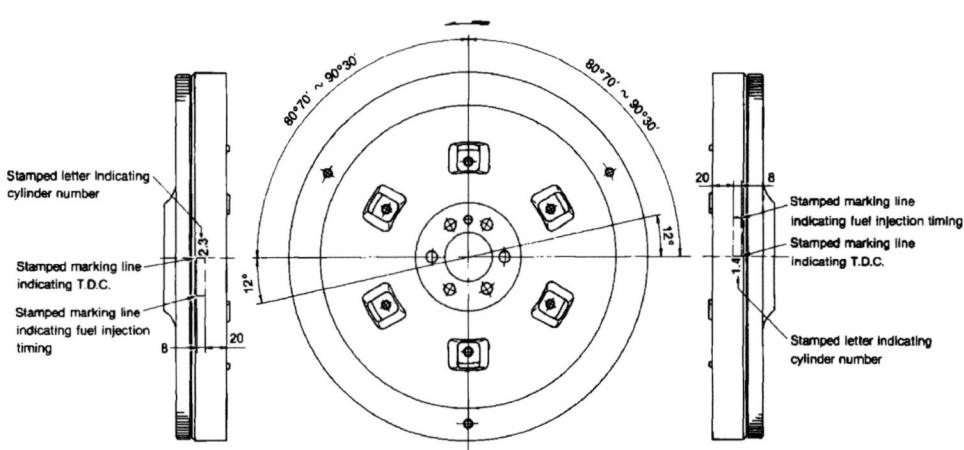

Printed in Japan
0000A0A1647

(2) Matching mark

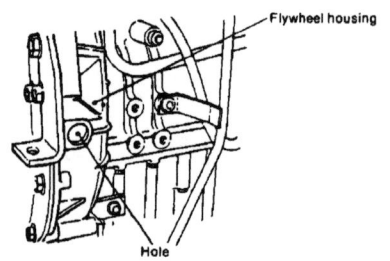

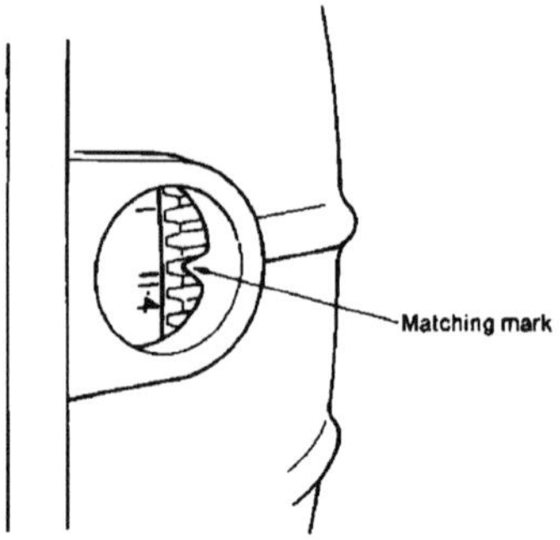

The matching mark is made at the hole of the flywheel housing.

9-5 Damper disc and cooling fan

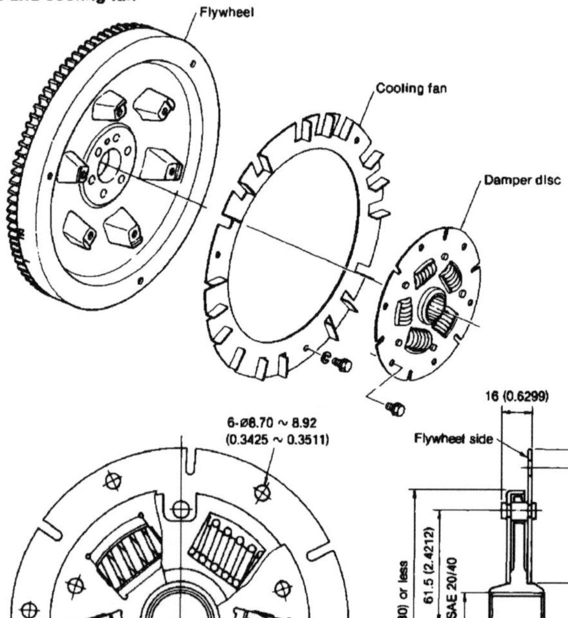

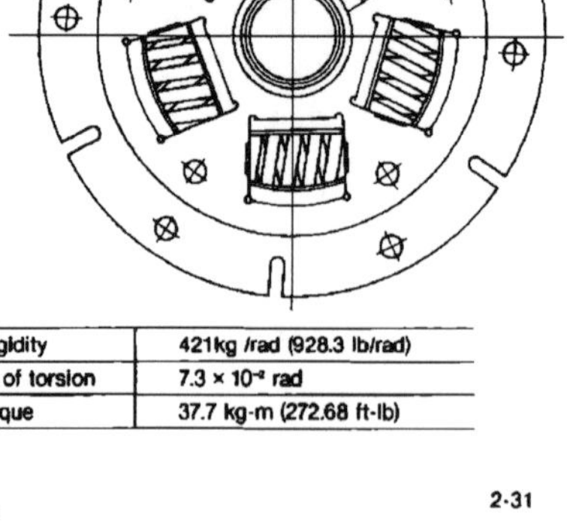

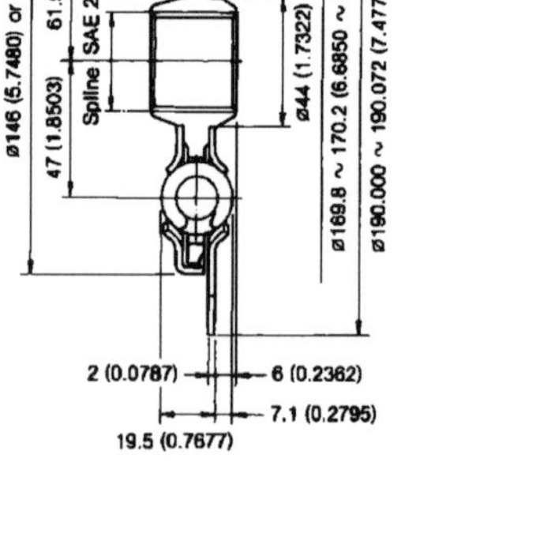

Torsional rigidity	421kg /rad (928.3 lb/rad)
Max. angle of torsion	7.3×10^{-2} rad
Stopper torque	37.7 kg-m (272.68 ft-lb)

CHAPTER 3
FUEL INJECTION EQUIPMENT

1. Fuel Supply System 3-1
2. Disassembly, Reassembly and Inspection
   of Governor 3-9
3. Disassembly, Reassembly and Inspection
   of Fuel Injection Pump 3-18
4. Adjustment of Fuel Injection
   Pump and Governor 3-28
5. Automatic Advancing Timer. 3-34
6. Fuel Feed Pump. 3-36
7. Fuel Injection Nozzle 3-38
8. Troubleshooting. 3-42
9. Fuel Injection Pump Service Data 3-44
10. Tools 3-45
11. Fuel Filter 3-47
12. Fuel Tank (Optional) 3-48
13. Design Change of Fuel Piping Line 3-49

Printed in Japan
0000A0A1647

Chapter 3 Fuel Injection Equipment
1. Fuel Supply System

1. Fuel Supply System

The Yanmar fuel injection pump is Bosch cluster type, the cam shaft of which is driven by the engine gears through the timing gear. The feed pump, driven by the cam shaft, pumps fuel oil from the fuel tank to the fuel filter at a pressure of 0.3kg/cm². The filtered fuel is supplied to the reservoir in the pump housing, the plunger increases the pressure, and the fuel goes through the injection pipe to be injected into each cylinder by the fuel injection nozzles.

IMPORTANT:
Automatic timer assembly, fuel injection nozzle assembly and injection pipe differ among engine models. When incorrect parts are installed, engine performance will drop.
Be sure to check the applicable engine model identification marks (I. D. Marks) provided on each part to insure use of the correct part.

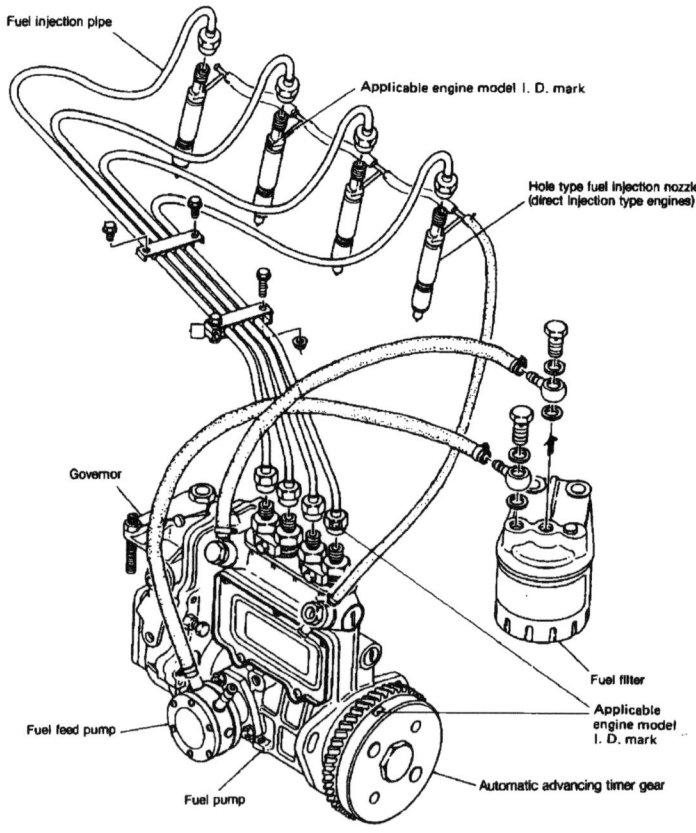

Chapter 3 Fuel Injection Equipment
1. Fuel Supply System

I. D. Marks for Automatic Timer Assembly

		I. D. Mark	Applicable Engine Model & E/#	
Automatic Timer Ass'y (Automatic Advancing Timer)	Old type	JH-A0	4JHE	E/# 00101 ~ 00574
		JH-A1	4JHE	E/# 01000 and before
		JH-B0	4JH-TE	E/# 11000 and before
		JH-C0	4JH-HTE	E/# 21000 and before
	New type	TN-A0	4JHE	E/# 01001 and after
		JH-C0	4JH-TE	E/# 11001 and after
			4JH-HTE	E/# 21001 and after
			4JH-DTE	E/# 30101 and after

I. D. Marks for Fuel Injection Nozzle Assembly and Fuel Injection Pipe

		I. D. Mark	Applicable Engine Model & E/#	Nozzle I. D. Mark
Fuel injection nozzle ass'y	Old type	A	4JHE	E/# 00101 ~ 00574	150P244J0
		E	4JHE	E/# 01000 and before	155P244J1
		B	4JH-TE	E/# 11000 and before	150P284J0
		D	4JH-HTE	E/# 21000 and before	145P265J1
	New type	F	4JHE	E/# 01001 and after	155P244J2
		G	4JH-TE	E/# 11001 and after	140P255J2
			4JH-HTE	E/# 21001 and after	
			4JH-DTE	E/# 30101 and after	

I. D. Marks for Fuel Injection Pipe

		I. D. Mark	Applicable Engine Model & E/#	Pipe Inner Dia
Fuel Injection Pipe (Pump to Nozzle)	Old type	None	4JHE	E/# 01000 and before	ϕ1.8
			4JH-TE	E/# 11000 and before	
		None	4JH-HTE	E/# 21000 and before	ϕ2.0
	New type	18	4JHE	E/# 01001 and after	ϕ1.8
			4JH-TE	E/# 11001 and after	
		20	4JH-HTE	E/# 21001 and after	ϕ2.0
			4JH-DTE	E/# 30101 and after	

Chapter 3 Fuel Injection Equipment
1. Fuel Supply System

1-1 Fuel injection pump construction

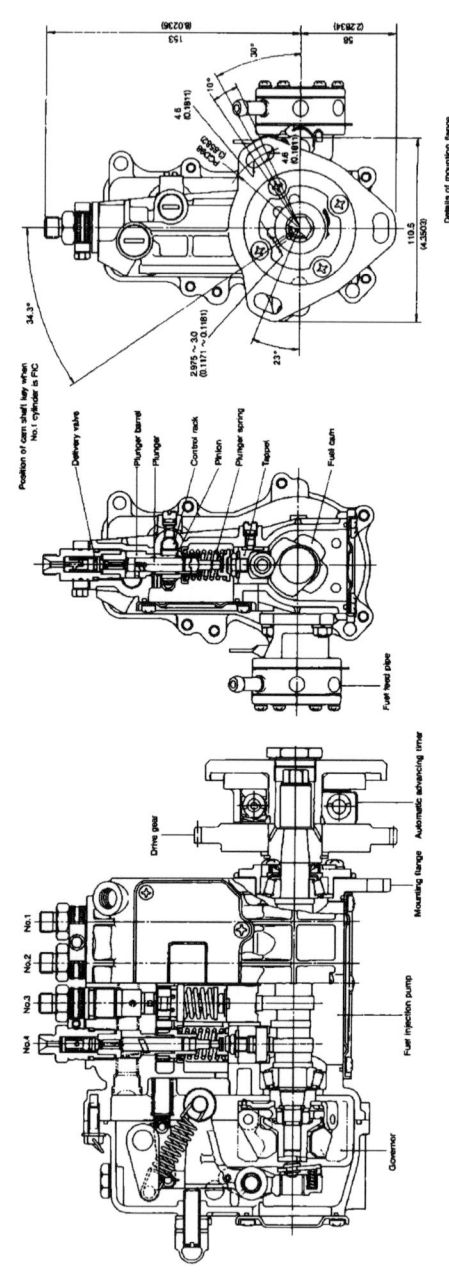

Chapter 3 Fuel Injection Equipment
1. Fuel Supply System

4JH Series

The Yanmar Model YPES Bosch type fuel injection pump is an in-line cluster type pump with a governor and timer incorporated.

A cam shaft is built into the fuel injection pump, which has a drive cam for the fuel supply pump and a tappet drive cam for the plunger. A timing gear and drive gear are mounted on the drive side of the cam shaft, and a governor weight on the opposite side.

As the plunger rises, the fuel oil opens the delivery valve and goes through the high pressure pipe to the fuel injection nozzles.

When the control rack connected to the governor lever moves, the pinion turns the plunger. This changes the fuel discharge and intake positions and in turn controls the amount of fuel injected.

1-2 Fuel injection pump specifications

Type		YPES-CL
No of cylinders		4
Plunger dia.	mm (in.)	8 (0.3149)
Cam lift	mm (in.)	7 (0.2755)
Max. fuel injection volume	mm³/st	65 (0.0039)
Max. fuel injection press.	kg/cm² (lb/in.²)	450 (6399)
Max. cam shaft	rpm	2200
Direction of revolution		right (looking from drive side)

1-3 Functioning of fuel injection pump

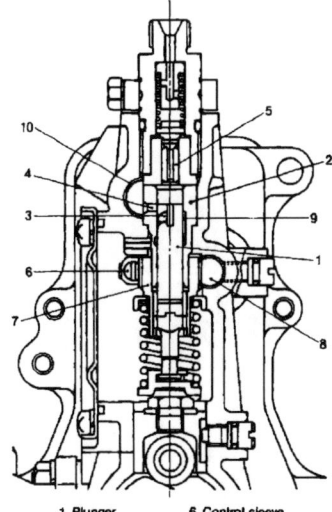

1. Plunger
2. Plunger barrel
3. Lead groove
4. Intake port
5. Delivery valve
6. Control sleeve
7. Control pinion
8. Control rack
9. Fuel leak return groove
10. Protector

The fuel injection pump supplies pressurized fuel to the injection nozzles through the action of the plunger. The plunger reciprocates in the plunger barrel through a fixed stroke and is lapped for a precise fit. A lead groove is helically cut in the plunger, and this leads to a connecting groove which goes to the top of the plunger.

There is a port in the plunger barrel which serves as both an intake and discharge port. The fuel comes through this port into the plunger chamber, is pressurized by the plunger, opens the delivery valve, flows to the fuel injection nozzle through the fuel injection pipe and is injected into the combustion chamber. Fuel injection terminates after the pressurized fuel has been discharged. This happens when the lead groove lines up with the discharge groove as the plunger rises and the pressure in the fuel injection pipe drops.

The control sleeve groove is fitted to the plunger flange. The control sleeve is secured to the control pinion and the pinion teeth and rack gear teeth are engaged.

The plunger is controlled by the rack, enabling continuous changing of the volume of fuel injected from zero to maximum. A fuel leak return hole is provided in the plunger barrel. This returns fuel leaking from the gap between the plunger and the barrel to the fuel lines. This prevents dilution of the lubricant in the cam chamber.

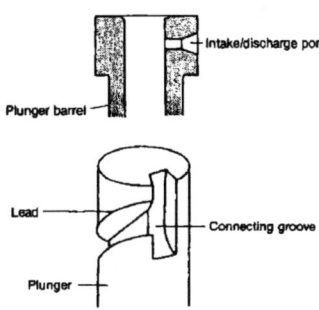

1-4 Injection volume control

(1) Full injection volume position
When the rack is set at the maximum setting, fuel injection starts earlier. It occurs when the widest part of the lead groove on the upper part of plunger lines up with the intake port in the barrel. At this time, the nar-

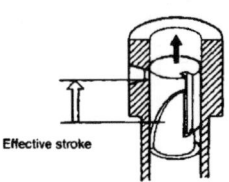

Effective stroke

Chapter 3 Fuel Injection Equipment
1. Fuel Supply System

rowest part of the lower lead groove lines up with the discharge port, prolonging the length of injection and increasing the volume of fuel injected.
This setting is normally used for starting and max. output operation.

(2) Half injection volume position
When the rack is returned towards zero from the maximum setting, discharge starts later and ends earlier, decreasing the volume of fuel injected.

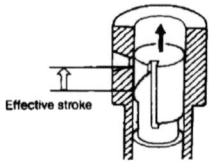
Effective stroke

(3) No fuel injection
When the rack is set near zero, the intake/discharge port in the barrel is always open, so no fuel is pressurized (even though the plunger continues to reciprocate).

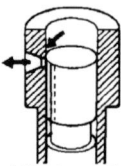

The delivery valve at the top of the plunger prevents fuel in the fuel injection pipe from flowing back to the plunger and sucks up fuel from the nozzle valve to prevent after drip.
When the plunger lead lines up with the discharge port of the plunger barrel, the injection pressure drops, and the delivery valve is brought down by the delivery valve spring.

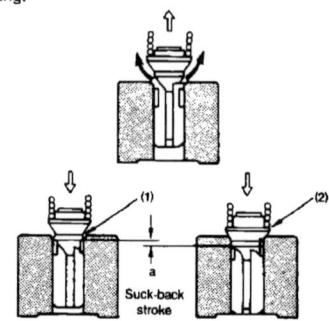
Suck-back stroke

At this time, the suck-back collar (1) blocks off the fuel injection pipe and the delivery chamber, and the valve continues to descend until the seat (2) comes in contact with the barrel. The fuel oil pressure in the fuel injection pipe decreases proportionately with the lowering of the valve (due to increased volume).
This accelerates closing of the nozzle valve, and sucks up fuel from the nozzle to prevent it from dripping.
This increases nozzle life and improves combustion efficiency.

1-5 Governor construction

Usage conditions of diesel engines are extremely varied, with a wide range of loads and rpms. The governor plays an important role in the operation of the engine by quickly adjusting the position of the control rack to control the amount of fuel injected according to changes in rpm.
It also automatically controls the engine to prevent engine rpm from exceeding the maximum, and keeps the engine from stopping.

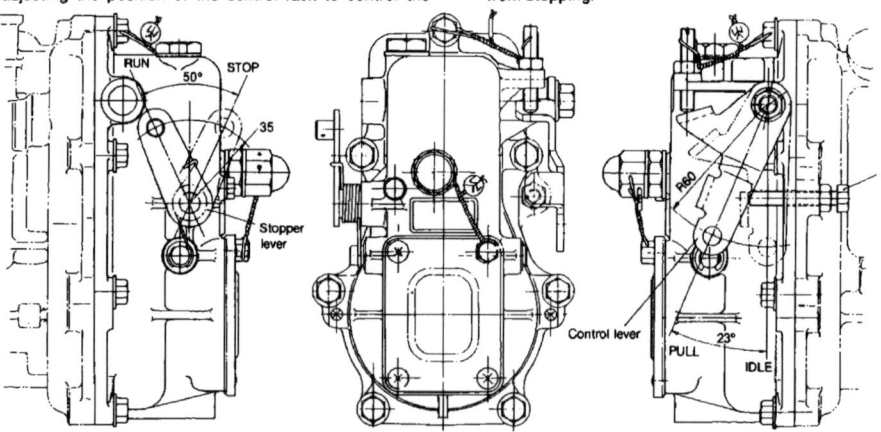

Chapter 3 Fuel Injection Equipment
1. Fuel Supply System

(1) A-type governor (without angleich spring)

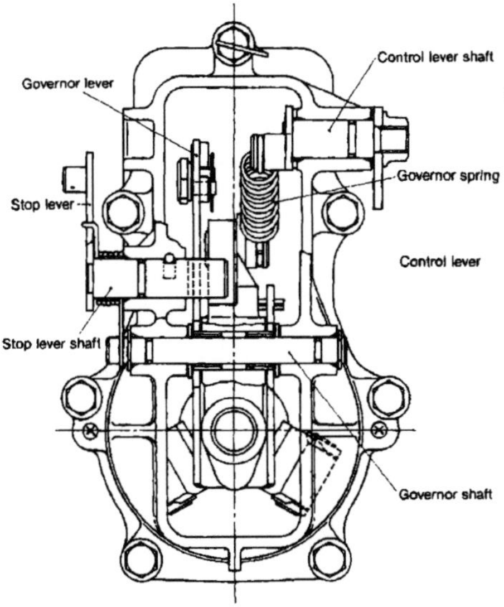

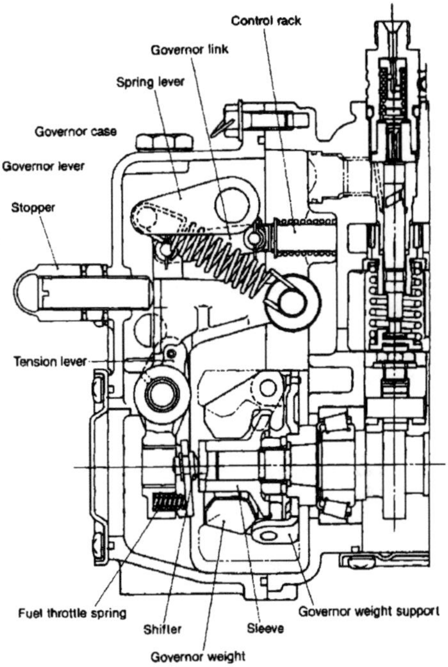

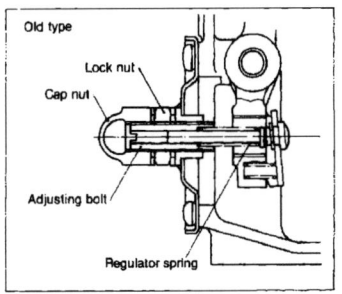

This governor is all-speed, directly connected to the YPES-CL fuel injection pump. The construction will be explained with the cutaway views.

The governor weight mounted on the end of the fuel injection pump cam shaft rotates around the governor support pin, driven by the cam shaft, and is forced outwards by the centrifugal force acting on the weight.

The thrust force acting on the cam shaft due to this centrifugal force acts on the lower part of the tension lever through the sleeve. A starting throttle spring is mounted on the bottom of the tension lever.
One end of the governor spring is hooked to the right upper end of the tension bar, and the other end to the spring lever of the control lever shaft.

As the spring lever and control lever are mounted on the same shaft, when the control lever is turned towards full, the governor spring is pulled and the load gradually increases.
As the lever is turned, the spring force acting on the upper end of the tension lever and the thrust force acting on the lower end of the tension lever come into equilibrium, to obtain the specified rpm.

Since the tension bar can move freely around the governor shaft on the player bearing, as rpm increases and the shifter is pushed to the left, the tension bar rotates clockwise, and when rpm decreases, the tension bar rotates counterclockwise.

Chapter 3 Fuel Injection Equipment
1. Fuel Supply System

4JH Series

The governor lever rotates smoothly on the same governor shaft. The bottom part of this lever is in contact with the sleeve through the shifter, which is in contact with the bottom of the tension lever through the throttle spring. It therefore moves with the tension lever according to increases/decreases in engine rpm.

The top of the governor is connected to the fuel pump control rack by a link. The movement of the lever controls the volume of fuel injected by the pump. When rpm increases the lever rotates clockwise to cause the control rack to reduce fuel, and when rpm decreases the lever rotates counterclockwise to cause the control rack to increase fuel, thus controlling engine rpm.

The top of the tension bar comes in contact with the stopper built into the top of the governor case to limit the maximum fuel injection volume.

Function of governor (on 4JH Series)

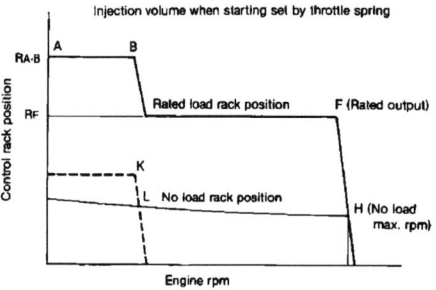

(1) Starting control

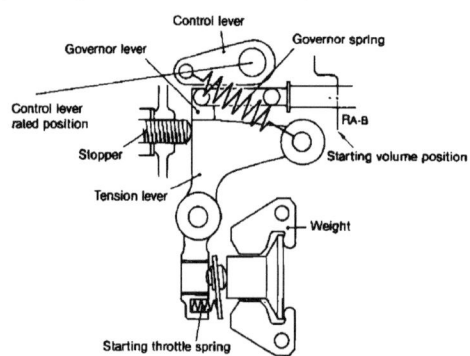

The control lever is set at the max. rpm position. The tension lever connected to the control lever is pulled as far as the stopper. The starting throttle spring mounted inbetween the tension lever and governor lever increases the governor weight thrust load, and the control rack is set at the max. injection volume position, to attain the starting volume.

(2) Idling control

Idling control is effected by the governor spring as this engine is not provided with an idling spring.
When the control lever is returned to the idling position after starting, almost no tension acts on the governor spring. The thrust force of the governor weight, and the starting throttle spring and governor spring load, come into equilibrium, effecting idling speed control.

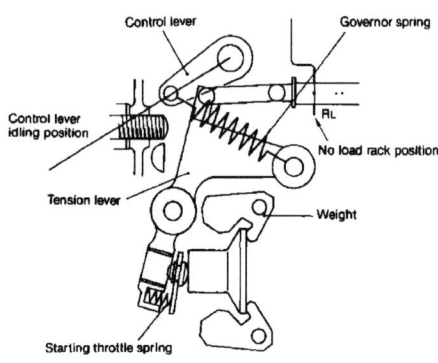

(3) Rated load max. rpm control

At rated load, the thrust load of the governor weight and the governor spring load are in equilibrium. The tension lever and governor lever come together and are limited by the stopper. The control rack is maintained at the position necessary for the rated load.

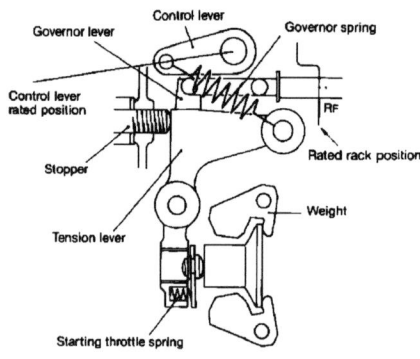

Chapter 3 Fuel Injection Equipment
1. Fuel Supply System

(4) No load max. rpm control
When rpm increases further from the max. load rpm control position, the thrust load of the governor weight exceeds that of the governor spring load, and causes the control rack to decrease injection volume through the tension lever and governor lever.

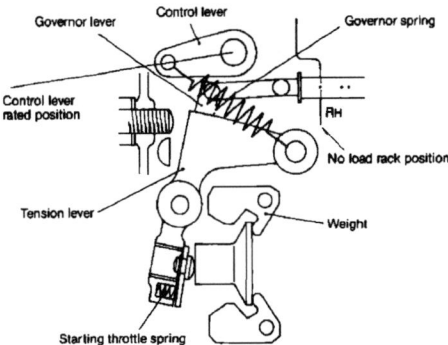

(5) Stopping engine
When you turn the stop handle, the governor causes the rack to decrease injection volume and stop the engine, regardless of the governor spring load.

2. Disassembly, Reassembly and Inspection of Governor

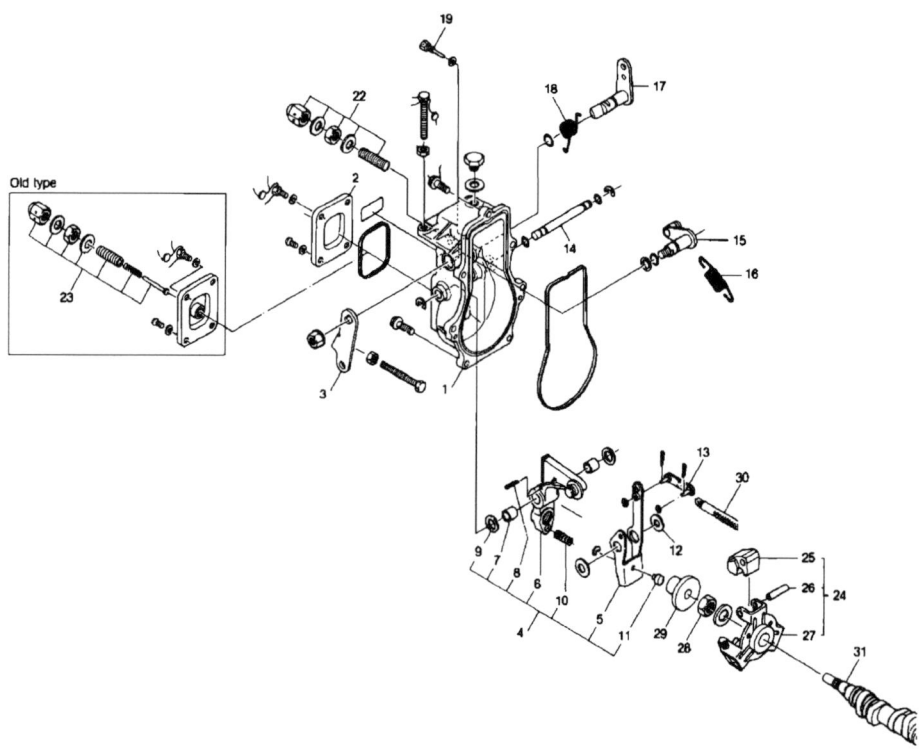

1. Governor case
2. Governor case cover
3. Control lever
4. Governor lever assembly 5. Governor lever
6. Tension lever
7. Bushing
8. Spring pin
9. Shim
10. Throttle spring
11. Shifter
12. Washer
13. Governor link
14. Governor shaft
15. Control lever shaft
16. Governor spring
17. Stop lever
18. Stop lever return spring
19. Stop lever stop pin
22. Fuel stopper (limit bolt) assembly
23. Adjusting spring assembly
24. Governor weight
25. Governor weight
26. Pin
27. Governor weight support
28. Governor weight nut
29. Governor sleeve
30. Control rack
31. Fuel pump cam shaft

2-1 Governor disassembly

(1) Remove the governor case.

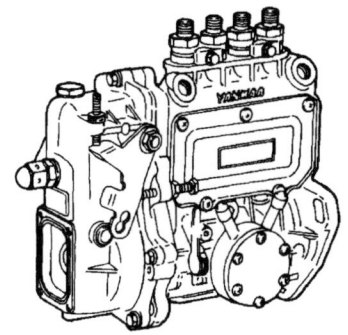

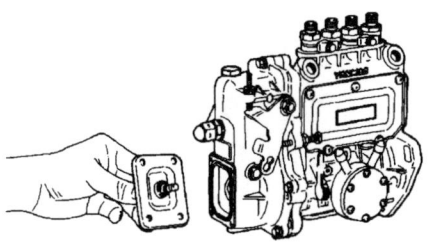

NOTE: Loosen the hex bolt on models with an angleich spring.

(2) Remove the control lever hex nut, and pull out the control lever from the control lever shaft.

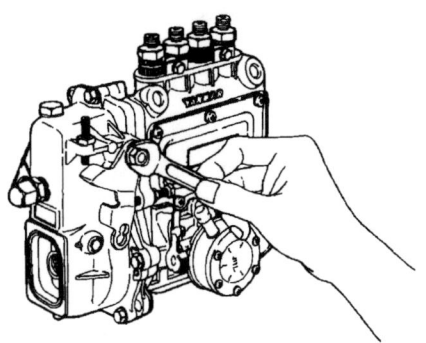

(3) Remove the governor case bolt. Remove the governor case (parallel pin) from the fuel pump unit while lightly tapping the governor case with a wood hammer. Create a gap between the governor case and fuel pump by moving only the moving parts of the governor lever.

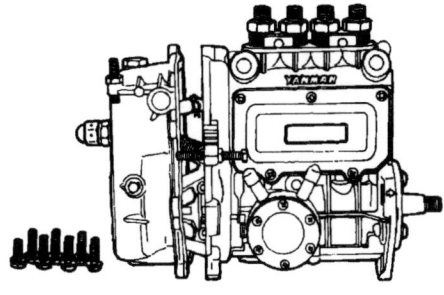

(4) Pull out the governor link snap pin by inserting needle nosed pliers between the fuel pump and governor case. case.

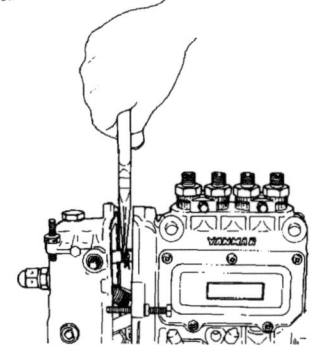

(5) The governor and fuel pump come apart by sliding the governor case and fuel pump apart and pulling out the link pin of the fuel control rack.

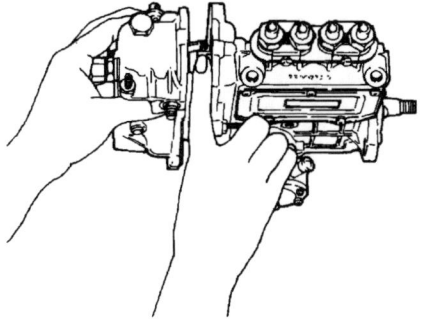

Chapter 3 Fuel Injection Equipment
2. Disassembly, Reassembly and Inspection of Governor

4JH Series

(8) Remove the snap-rings on both ends of the governor lever shaft.

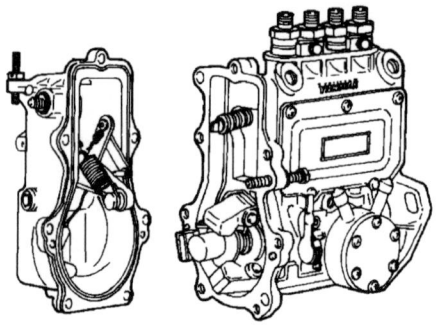

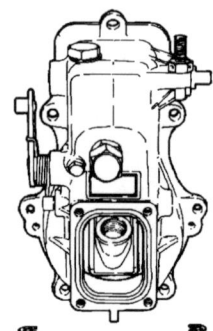

(6) Remove the stop lever return spring from the governor lever shaft.

(9) Put a rod 8mm (0.3150in.) in dia. or less in one end of the governor lever shaft, and tap the governor shaft until the O-ring comes out the other side of the governor case.

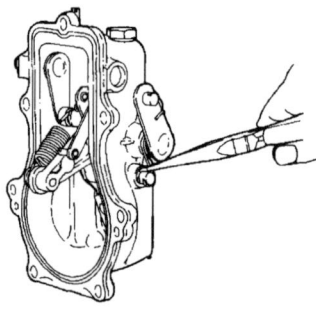

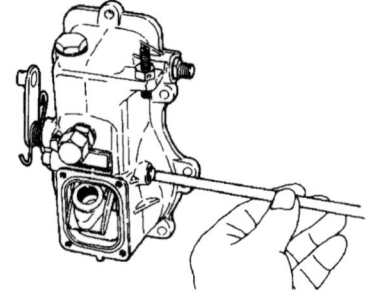

(7) Use needle nose pliers to unhook the governor spring from the tension lever and control lever shaft.

(10) After you remove the O-ring, lightly tap the end of the shaft that you removed the O-ring from, and remove the governor lever shaft. Then remove the governor shaft assembly and washer.

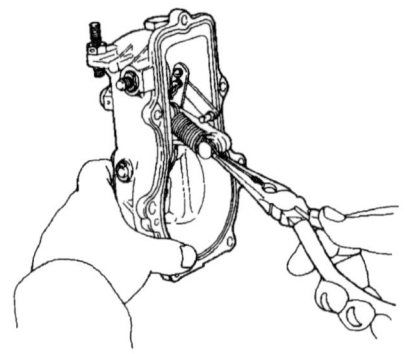

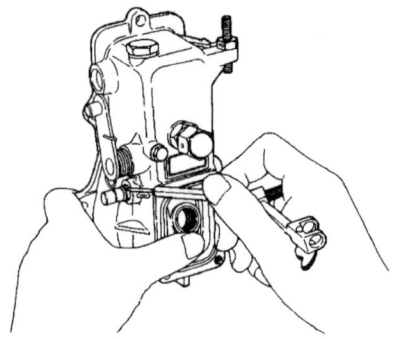

Chapter 3 Fuel Injection Equipment
2. Disassembly, Reassembly and Inspection of Governor

4JH Series

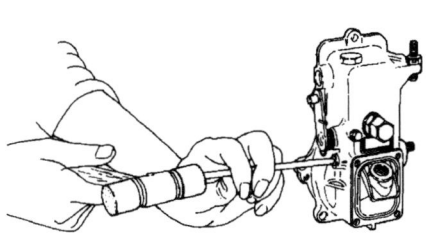

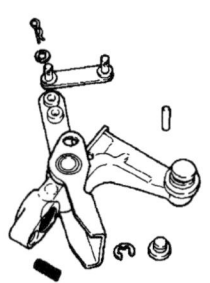

NOTE: *The governor assembly consists of the governor lever, tension bar, bushing, throttle spring and shifter, and is normally not disassembled.*
The spring pin is removed when you replace the shifter or throttle spring.

(12) When you need to pull out the stop lever, remove the stop lever shaft stop pin, and lightly tap the inside of the governor case.

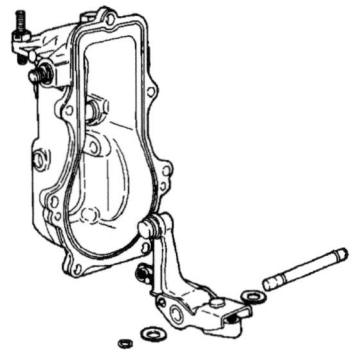

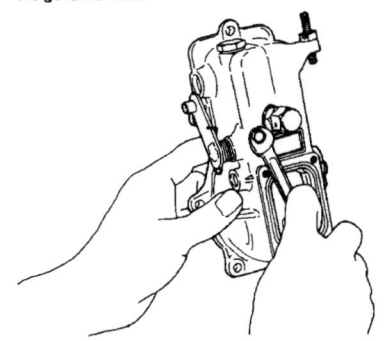

(11) Remove the governor link from the governor lever.

(13) When you need to pull out the control lever shaft, tap the end of the shaft with a wood hammer.

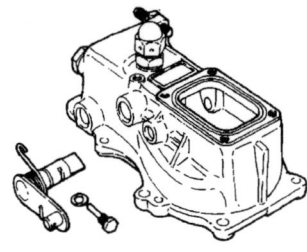

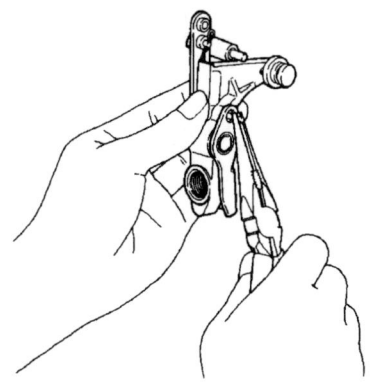

NOTE: 1. *Do not remove the fuel limit nut from the governor case unless necessary.*

Chapter 3 Fuel Injection Equipment
2. Disassembly, Reassembly and Inspection of Governor

4JH Series

(14) Pull out the governor sleeve on the end of the fuel camshaft by hand.

(16) Remove the governor weight assembly from the fuel pump cam using the governor weight pulling tools.

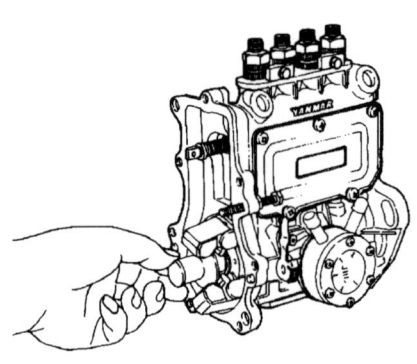

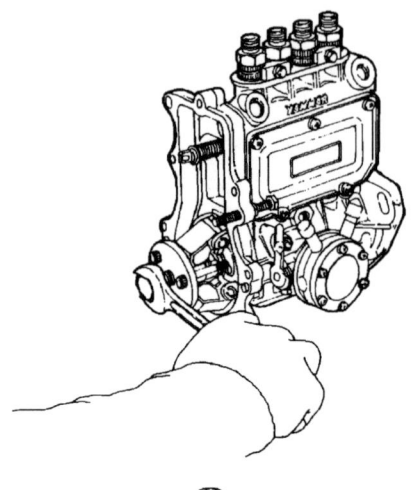

(15) Turn the governor weight with a box spanner two or three times to loosen it, stopping it with the hole in the fuel coupling ring or holding the coupling with a vise.

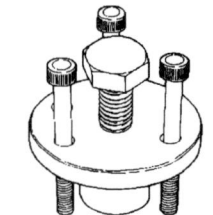

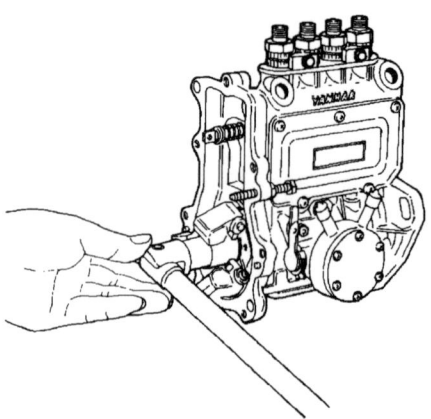

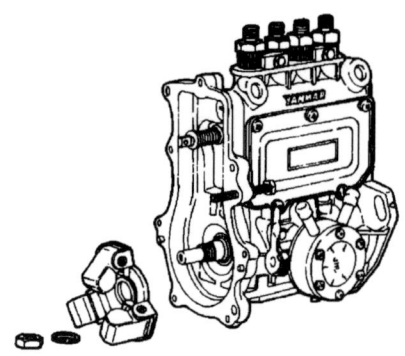

NOTE: When the taper fit comes apart after you have removed the nut, the governor weight may fly out —Be Careful.

NOTE: The governor weight assembly is made up of the governor weight, support and pin. Do not disassemble.

Chapter 3 Fuel Injection Equipment
2. Disassembly, Reassembly and Inspection of Governor ─────── 4JH Series

2-2 Inspection of governor

Inspection of governor weight assembly
(1) Replace the governor weight if it does not open and close smoothly.

(2) Replace the governor weight if the contact surface with governor sleeve is extremely worn.
(3) Replace if there is governor weight support/pin wear or the caulking is loose.
(4) Replace if the governor weight support stopper is excessively worn.

Inspection of governor sleeve

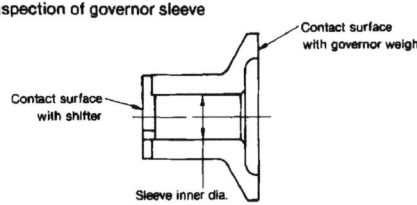

(1) Replace the governor sleeve if the contact surface with governor weight is worn or there is pitching.
(2) Replace the governor sleeve if the contact surface with shifter is considerably worn or there is pitching.
(3) If the governor sleeve does not move smoothly above the cam shaft due to governor sleeve inner dia. wear or other reasons, replace.

Inspection of governor shaft assembly
(1) Measure the clearance between the governor shaft and bushing, and replace if it exceeds the limit.

mm (in.)

	Standard Dimension	Standard Clearance	Limit
Governor shaft outer dia.	7.986 ~ 7.995 (0.3144 ~ 0.3147)	0.065 ~ 0.124 (0.0025 ~ 0.0048)	0.5 (0.0196)
Bushing inner dia.	8.060 ~ 8.110 (0.3173 ~ 0.3192)		

(2) Inspect the shifter contact surface, and replace the shifter (always by removing the pin to disassemble) if it is worn or scorched.
(3) Disassemble and replace throttle springs that are settled, broken or corroded by pulling the spring pin.
(4) Check link parts for bends or kinks that will cause malfunctioning, and replace any parts as necessary.

NOTE: 1. Side gap on top of governor lever shaft.

mm (in.)

Standard side gap	0.4 (0.0157)

2. Replace the governor lever, tension bar, bushing, shifter and throttle spring as an assembly.

(5) Inspection of springs
1) Check the governor spring and other springs and replace if they are broken, settled or corroded.
2) Measure the free length of the governor spring, and replace if it exceeds the limit.
See service data sheet for free length of governor spring.

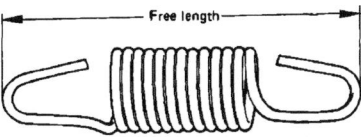

Governor spring spec. table

Engine model		4JHE, 4JH-TE	4JH-HTE, 4JH-DTE
Part No.		129470-61700	129473-61700
Spring constant	kg/mm	0.479	0.431
Free length	mm	54.0	52.5

2-3 Assembling governor

Inspect all parts after disassembly and replace any parts as necessary. Before starting reassembly, clean new parts and parts to be reused, and put them in order.
Make sure to readjust the unit after reassembly to obtain the specified performance.

(1) Insert the governor weight assembly in the taper portion at the end of the fuel pump camshaft, stopping it with the hole in the fuel coupling ring or holding the coupling with a vise, mount the rest, and tighten the governor weight nut.

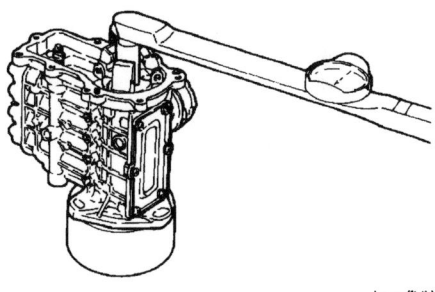

	kg-m (ft-lb)
Governor weight nut tightening torque	4.5 ~ 5.0 (32.54 ~ 36.16)

3-14

Printed in Japan
0000A0A1647

(2) Open the governor weight to the outside, and insert the sleeve in the end of the fuel pump camshaft.

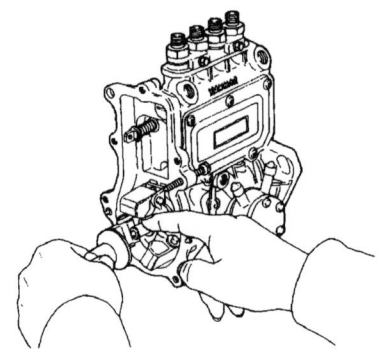

NOTE: Make sure that the sleeve moves smoothly after inserting it.

(3) When the stop lever has been disassembled, mount the stop lever return spring on the stop lever, tap the stop lever lightly with a wooden hammer to insert it, and tighten the stop lever stop pin.

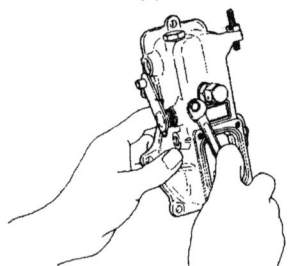

(4) When the control lever shaft has been removed, lightly tap the control lever shaft and washer from inside the governor case, using an appropriate plate.

(5) If the governor has been disassembled, tap in the spring pin.

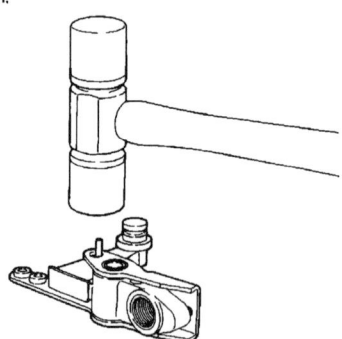

(6) Mount the governor lever assembly to the governor link.

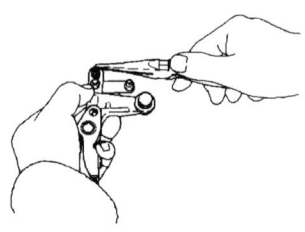

NOTE: 1. Make sure that the correct governor link mounting holes are used, and that it is mounted in the correct direction.
2. Make sure that the governor link moves smoothly.

(7) Put the governor lever shaft assembly in the governor case, insert the governor lever shaft, and tap it in until the O-ring groove comes out the opposite side of the governor case.

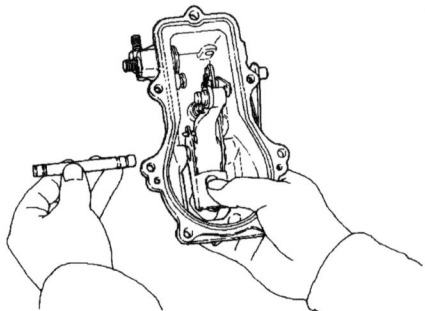

NOTE: 1. Fit the O-ring to the side you have tapped in.

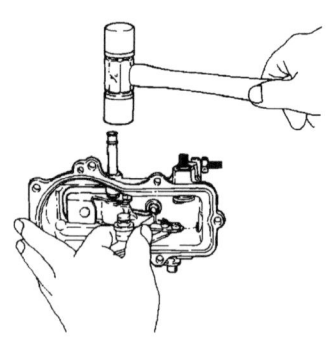

2. Make sure to insert the governor lever shaft in the correct direction.

Chapter 3 Fuel Injection Equipment
2. Disassembly, Reassembly and Inspection of Governor

4JH Series

3. Don't forget to mount the washers to both sides of the governor lever.

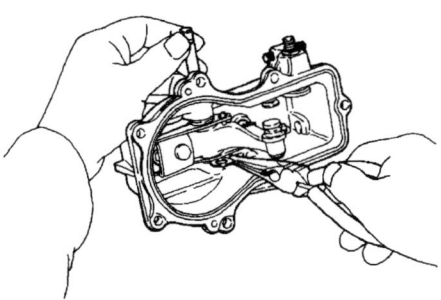

(8) After you have mounted the O-ring, tape the governor lever in the opposite direction, and mount the E-shaped stop rings on the grooves at both ends.

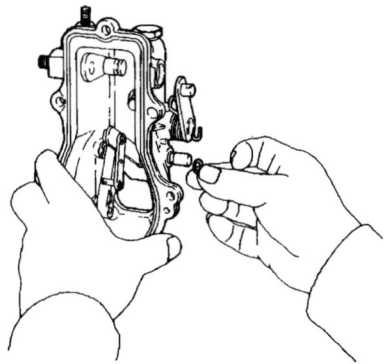

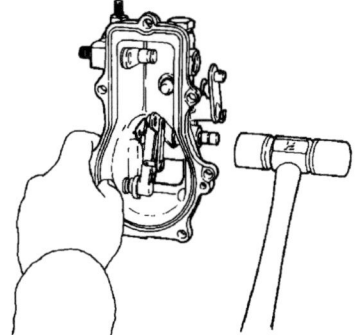

NOTE: After mounting the governor lever assembly, make sure the governor lever assembly moves smoothly.

(9) Fit the stop lever return spring to the end of the governor lever shaft.

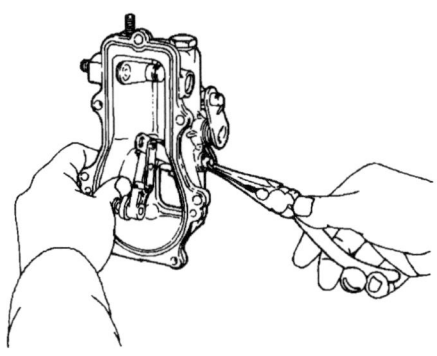

(10) Hook the governor spring on the control lever shaft and tension lever hook with radio pliers.

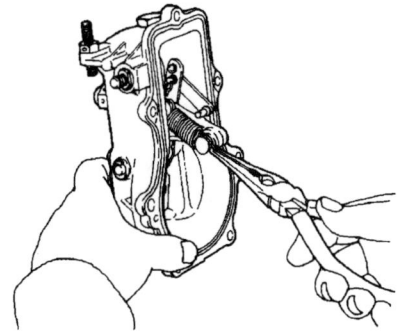

(11) Pull the governor link as far as possible towards the governor case mounting surface, insert the governor link pin in the fuel control rack pin hole and fit the snap pin on it.

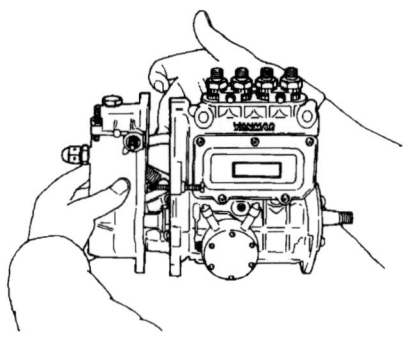

Chapter 3 Fuel Injection Equipment
2. Disassembly, Reassembly and Inspection of Governor

(12) Mount the governor case to the fuel pump unit while lightly tapping it with a wooden hammer, and tighten the bolts.
(13) Place the adjusting spring and adjusting rod on the governor case cover adjusting bolt, and mount the governor case cover.

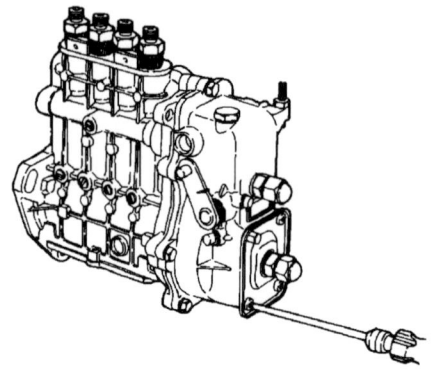

(14) Insert the control lever in the control lever shaft, and tighten the nut.

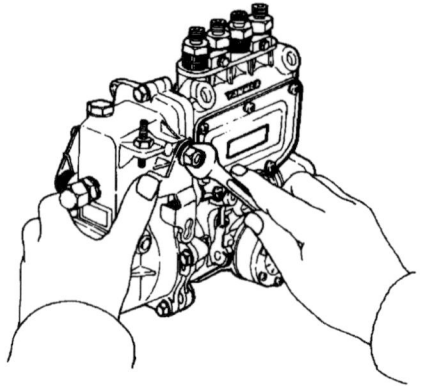

NOTE: Move the control lever back and forth to make sure that the entire link moves smoothly.

3. Disassembly, Reassembly and Inspection of Fuel Injection Pump

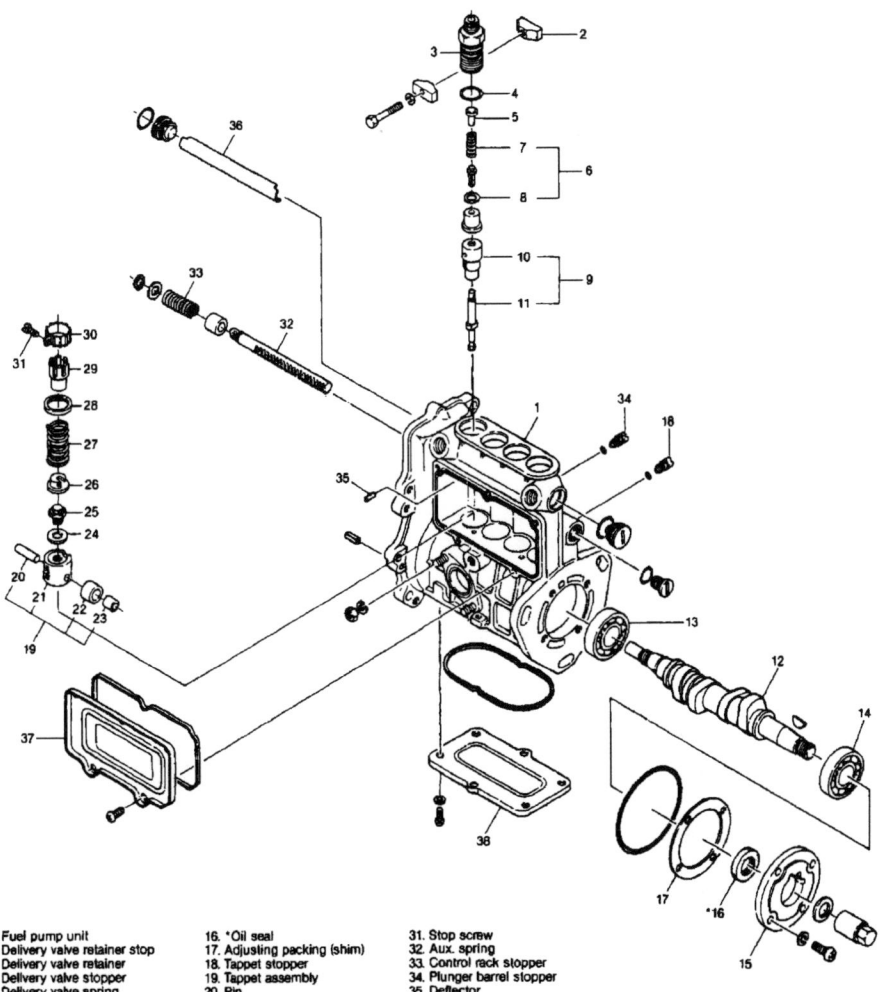

1. Fuel pump unit
2. Delivery valve retainer stop
3. Delivery valve retainer
4. Delivery valve stopper
5. Delivery valve spring
6. Delivery valve assembly
7. Delivery valve
8. Delivery valve seat
9. Plunger assembly
10. Plunger barrel
11. Plunger
12. Fuel pump camshaft
13. Bearing
14. Bearing
15. Bearing holder
16. *Oil seal
17. Adjusting packing (shim)
18. Tappet stopper
19. Tappet assembly
20. Pin
21. Roller guide
22. Roller (outer)
23. Roller (inner)
24. Adjusting shim
25. Adjusting bolt
26. Plunger spring rest B
27. Plunger spring
28. Plunger spring rest A
29. Control sleeve (reduction ring)
30. Control pinion B
31. Stop screw
32. Aux. spring
33. Control rack stopper
34. Plunger barrel stopper
35. Deflector
36. Pump side cover
37. Pump bottom cover

NOTE: 1. Some models are equipped with ball bearings and some with taper roller bearings.

2. *Oil seal: Some models are equipped with oil seals and some are not. The shape of the bearing holder differs for models with and without oil seals.

Chapter 3 Fuel Injection Equipment
3. Disassembly, Reassembly and Inspection of Fuel Injection Pump _____ 4JH Series

3-1 Disassembly of fuel injection pump
When disassembling the fuel pump, separate the parts for each cylinder and be careful not to get them mixed up. Be especially careful to keep the plunger/plunger barrel, delivery valve/delivery valve seat and other assemblies separate for each cylinder (the parts of each assembly must be kept with that assembly and put back in the same cylinder).

Preparation
1. Wash off the dirt and grease on the outside of the pump with cleaning oil (kerosene or diesel oil) before disassembly.
2. Perform work in a clean area.
3. Take off the fuel pump bottom cover and remove lubricant oil.
4. Turn the fuel pump upside down to drain fuel oil.

(2) Remove the fuel feed pump.
NOTE: *Do not disassemble the fuel feed pump. See instructions for fuel feed pump for details.*

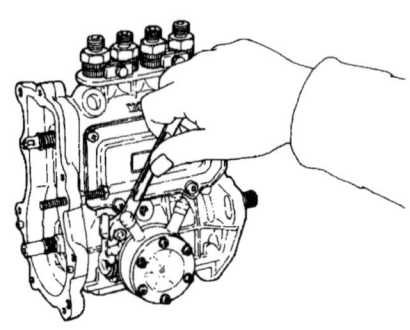

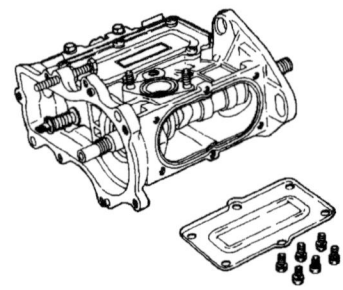

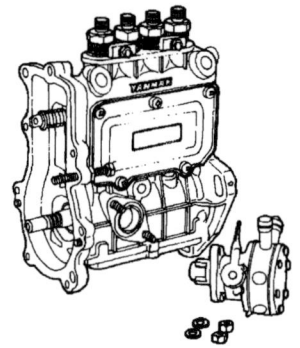

(1) Loosen the nut with a box spanner and take it off, holding it with the hole in the fuel coupling ring or holding the coupling with a vise and take out the governor weight assembly.

(3) Remove the fuel pump side cover.

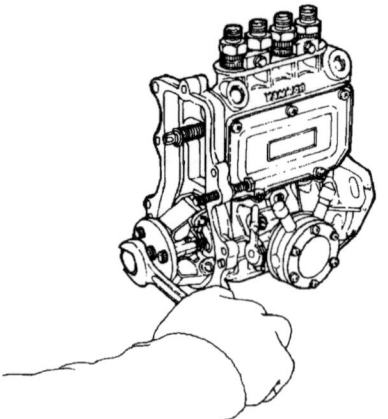

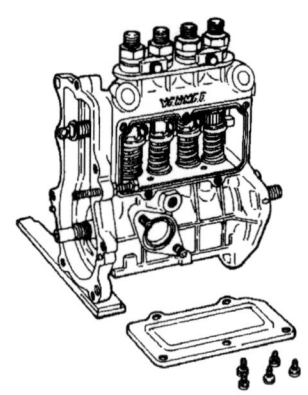

Chapter 3 Fuel Injection Equipment
3. Disassembly, Reassembly and Inspection of Fuel Injection Pump — 4JH Series

(4) Turn the camshaft until the roller guide is at the maximum head, and insert the plunger spring support plate in between the plunger spring washer B (lower side) and fuel pump unit.

(7) Turn the fuel pump upside down, move all the roller guides to the plunger side, and then put the pump on its side. Turn the camshaft to a position so that none of the cylinder cams hit the tappets.

(8) Put a plate against the governor end side of the camshaft and lightly tap it, and pull out the camshaft and drive side bearing.

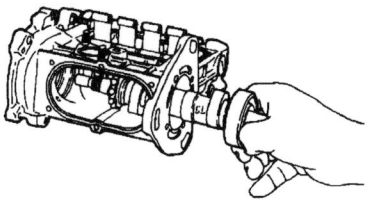

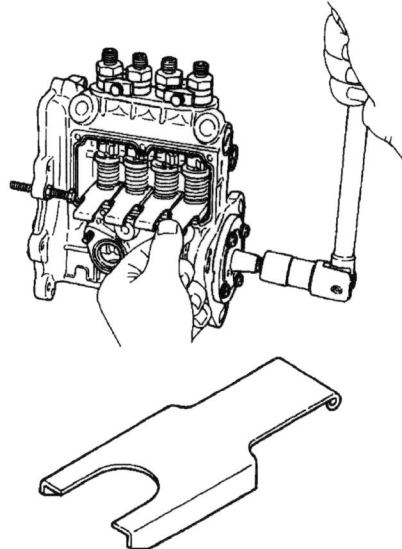

(9) Remove the roller guide stop.

Plunger spring support plate

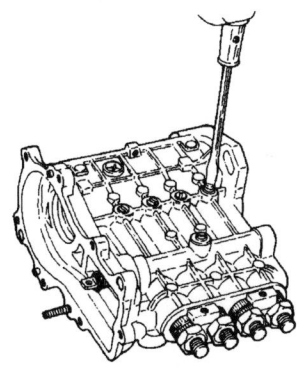

NOTE: If the camshaft does not turn, put double nuts on the end of the cam shaft or remove the coupling.

(5) Remove the camshaft wood ruff key.
(6) Put a screwdriver in the two grooves on the camshaft bearing holder mounting surface, and pull out the camshaft bearing holder.

(10) Use a hammer handle or the like to push up the roller guide from the bottom of the pump, and remove the plunger spring support plate.

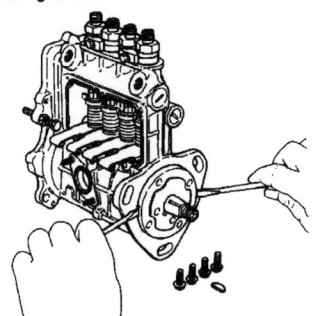

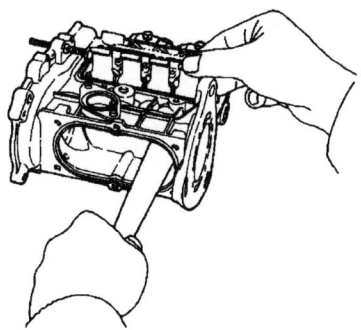

NOTE: 1. Make sure not to damage the oil seal with the threaded part of the camshaft.
2. Be careful not to loose the shims in between the pump and bearing holder.

NOTE: The plunger spring may make the roller guide and plunger, etc. fly out when the plunger support plate is removed.

3-20

Printed in Japan
0000A0A1647

Chapter 3 Fuel Injection Equipment
3. Disassembly, Reassembly and Inspection of Fuel Injection Pump
4JH Series

(11) Remove the roller guide.

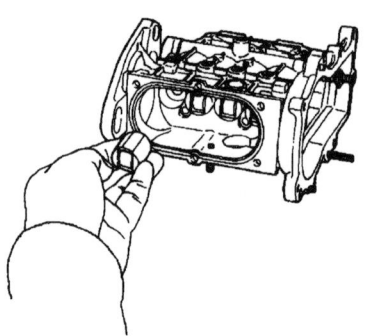

NOTE: When you stand the fuel pump up, all of the roller guides drop out at one time. Therefore, first remove the stop bolt for one cylinder at a time, and then the roller guide for each cylinder—continue this process.

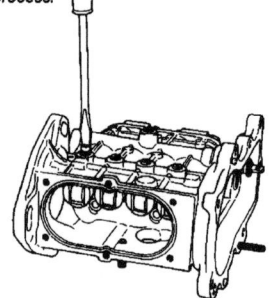

(12) Remove the plunger, plunger spring and lower washer from the lower part of the pump.

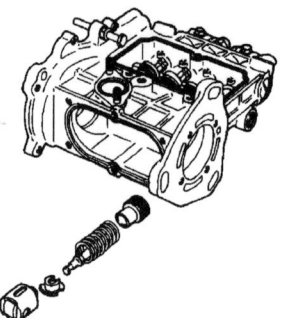

NOTE: Keep the parts separate for each cylinder.

(13) Loosen the small screw on control pinion.

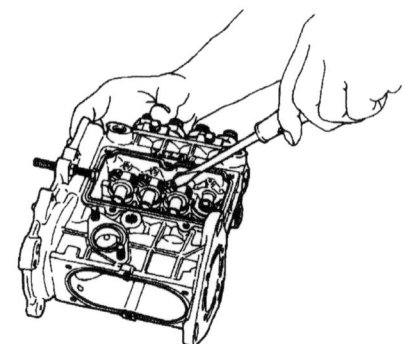

NOTE: 1. Check to make sure the match marks on the pinion/sleeve are correct before loosening the small screw on the control pinion, as the pinion and sleeve come apart when the screw is loosened. If the mark is hard to read or off center, lightly inscribe a new mark. This will serve as a guide when adjusting injection volume later.

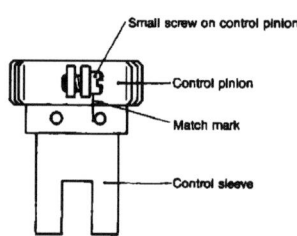

2. Keep parts separate for each cylinder.

(14) Remove the control pinion, sleeve and upper rest.

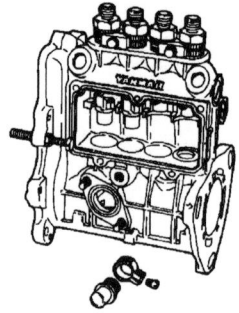

NOTE: Keep parts separate for each cylinder.

3-21

Printed in Japan

Chapter 3 Fuel Injection Equipment
3. Disassembly, Reassembly and Inspection of Fuel Injection Pump

4JH Series

(15) Remove the control rack stop bolt and remove the rack.

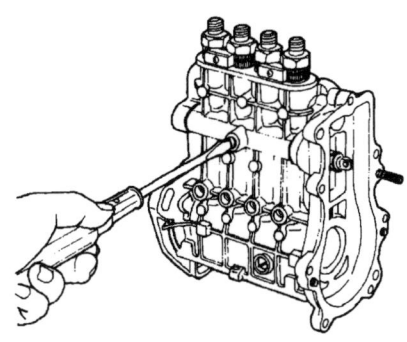

NOTE: Be careful not to lose the spring or rest on the control rack.

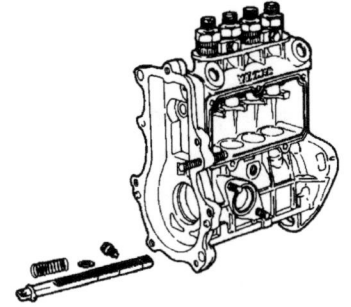

(16) Loosen the delivery valve retainer stop bolt, and remove the delivery valve holder stop.

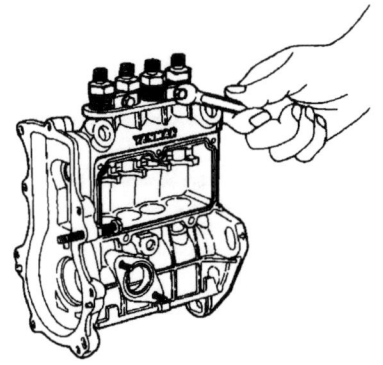

(17) Remove the delivery valve holder.

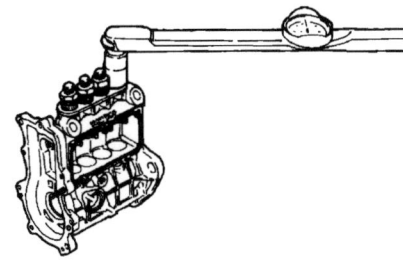

(18) Remove the delivery valve assembly.

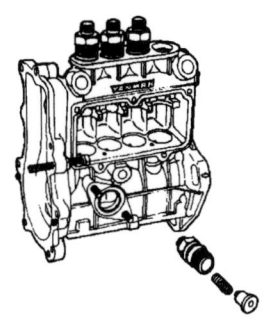

NOTE: 1. Be careful not to lose the delivery valve packing, delivery valve spring, delivery valve stopper or other small parts.
2. Keep the delivery valve assemblies for each cylinder clearly separated.

(19) Take the plunger barrel out from the top of pump.

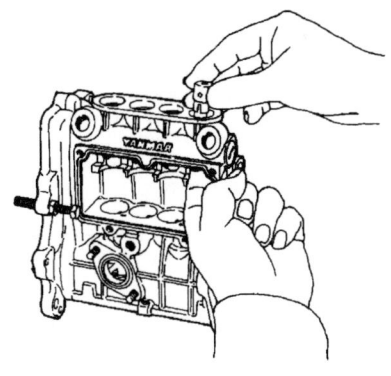

NOTE: Keep it as a set with the plunger that was removed earlier.

Chapter 3 Fuel Injection Equipment
3. Disassembly, Reassembly and Inspection of Fuel Injection Pump

4JH Series

3-2 Inspection of fuel injection pump
(1) Inspection of plunger
  1) Thoroughly wash the plungers, and replace plungers that have scratches on the plunger lead or are discolored.
  2) The plunger is in good condition if it slides down smoothly when it is tilted about 60°. Repeat this several times while turning the plunger. Repair or replace if it slides down too quickly or if it stops part way.

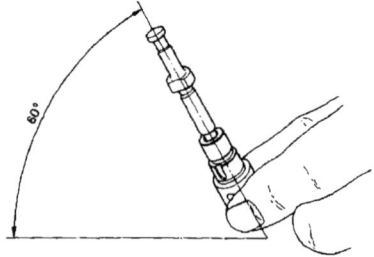

(2) Inspection of delivery valve

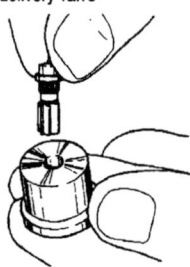

1) Replace as a set if the delivery valve suck-back collar or seat are scratched, scored, scuffed, worn, etc.
2) The valve is in good condition if it returns when released after being pushed it down with your finger (while the holes in the bottom of the delivery guide seat are covered). Replace if necessary.
3) Likewise, the valve should completely close by its own weight when you take your finger off the holes in the bottom of the delivery guide sheet.

NOTE: When fitting new parts, wash with diesel oil and perform the above inspection.

(3) Inspection of pump
  1) Inspect for extreme wear of roller guide sliding surface. Scratches on the roller pin sliding surface are not a problem.
  2) Inspect the plunger barrel seat.
     If there are burrs or discoloration, repair or replace as this will lead to dilution of the lubricant.
(4) Inspection of fuel camshaft and bearings
  1) Fuel camshaft
     Inspect for scratches or wear of camshaft, deformation of key grooves and deformation of screws on both ends, and replace if necessary.
  2) Bearings
     Replace if the taper rollers or outer race surface is flaked or worn.

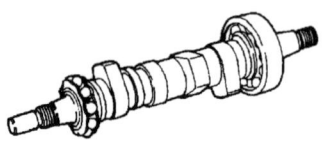

NOTE: Replace fuel camshafts and bearings together.

(5) Inspection of roller guide assembly
  1) Roller

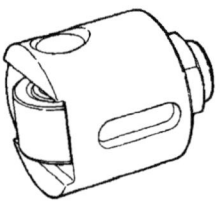

Replace if the surface is worn or flaked.
  2) Roller Guide
     Replace if the outer roller pin hole is extensively worn or there are many scratches.
  3) Replace if the play of the roller guide assembly pin/roller is 0.2mm (0.0078in.) or more.
  4) Injection timing adjustment bolt
     Replace if the surface in contact with the plunger side is unevenly or excessively worn.
(6) Inspection of rack and pinion
  1) Rack

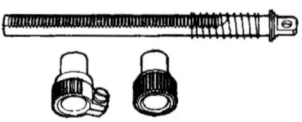

Inspect for bending of rack and wear or deformation of fit with pinion.
  2) Pinion
     Inspect for wear or deformation of fit with rack.

NOTE: If the tooth surface or sliding surface is not in good working order, rack resistance increases, affecting the condition of the engine (rough rpm, over running, etc.).

(7) Inspection of plunger spring and delivery spring
    Inspect springs for scratches, cracks, breakage, uneven wear and rust.

Chapter 3 Fuel Injection Equipment
3. Disassembly, Reassembly and Inspection of Fuel Injection Pump
4JH Series

(8) Inspection of oil seals
Inspect oil seals to see if they are burred or scratched.
(9) Inspection of roller guide stop
Inspect the side of the tip, replace if excessively worn.
(10) Inspection of O-rings
Inspect and replace if they are burred or cracked.

3-3 Reassembly of fuel injection pump

Preparation
After inspection, put all parts in order and clean.
See Inspection of Fuel Pump for inspection procedure.

(1) Put in the plunger barrel from the top of pump.

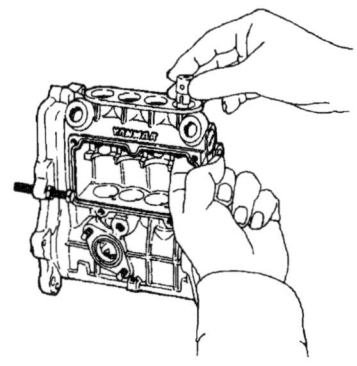

NOTE: Make sure the barrel key groove is fitted properly to the barrel stop pin.

(2) Place the delivery valve assembly, packing, spring and stopper from the top of the pump, in this order.

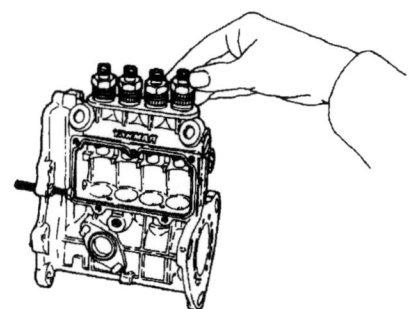

NOTE: Replace the delivery valve packing and O-ring.

(3) Place the control rack, and tighten the control rack stop bolt.

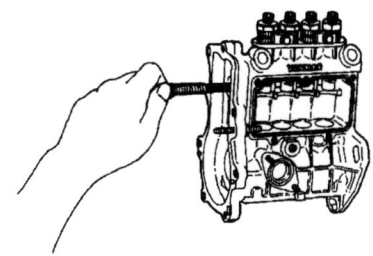

NOTE: 1. Do not forget the rack aux. spring.
2. Make sure the rack moves smoothly through a full cycle.

(4) Place the rack set screw (using the special tool) in the rack stop bolt screw hole to fix the rack.
(5) Looking from the bottom of pump, align the match marks on the rack and pinion.

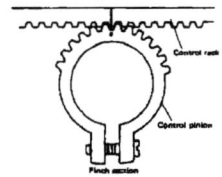

(6) While holding the pinion with one hand and keeping it aligned with the match mark, fit in the sleeve, and lightly tighten the small pinion screw.

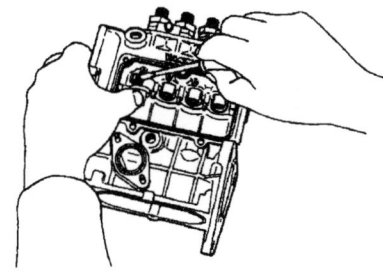

NOTE: Fitting of sleeve; Face towards small pinion screws and align with match mark.

Pinion/sleeve match mark

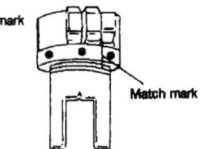

3-24

Printed in Japan
0000A0A1647

Chapter 3 Fuel Injection Equipment
3. Disassembly, Reassembly and Inspection of Fuel Injection Pump
4JH Series

(7) Mount the plunger spring upper rest.

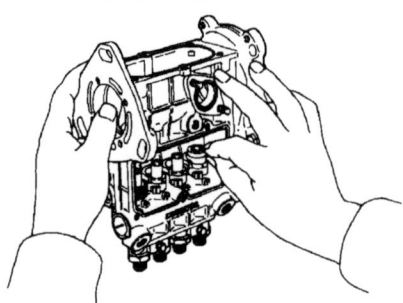

NOTE: 1. Make sure to mount the upper rest with the hollow side facing down.
2. Recheck to make sure that the rack moves easily.

(8) Mount the plunger spring.
(9) Mount the lower rest on the head of the plunger, and fit the plunger in the lower part of pump while aligning the match marks on the plunger flange and the sleeve.

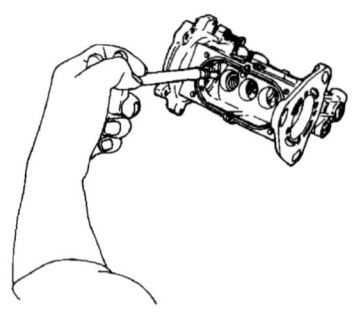

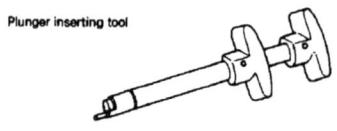

Plunger inserting tool

NOTE: If the plunger is mounted in the opposite direction, the injection volume will increase abnormally and cannot be adjusted.

(10) Insert the plunger spring support plate between the plunger spring seat B (lower) and fuel pump, by putting the handle of a hammer in the lower part of pump and pushing the roller guide up.

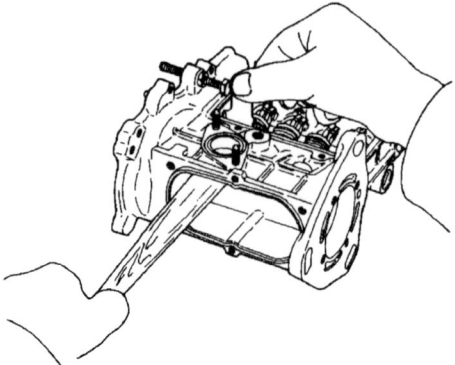

NOTE: 1. Face the roller guide stop groove up, and align with stop screw hole on pump.

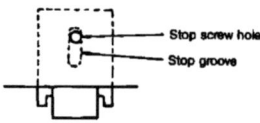

Stop screw hole
Stop groove

2. Check movement of rack. The plunger spring may be out of place if movement is heavy—insert a screwdriver and bring to correct position.
3. When replacing the roller guide assembly, fit shims and lightly tighten:

Standard shim thickness	1.2 mm (0.0472 in.)
Part code number	129155-51600

(11) Make sure that roller guide stop groove is in correct position, and tighten roller guide stop bolt.

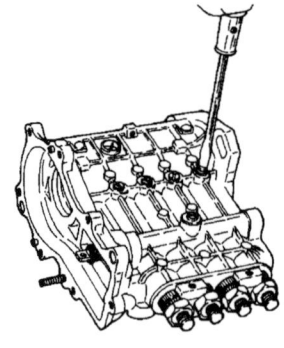

Chapter 3 Fuel Injection Equipment
3. Disassembly, Reassembly and Inspection of Fuel Injection Pump — 4JH Series

(12) Fit the bearings to both ends of the camshaft, and insert from drive side by lightly tapping.

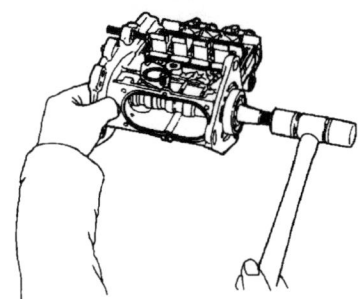

NOTE: Turn pump upside down, and tap camshaft in while moving roller guide to plunger spring side.

(13) Fit the oil seal on the inside of the bearing retainer and mount the bearing retainer.

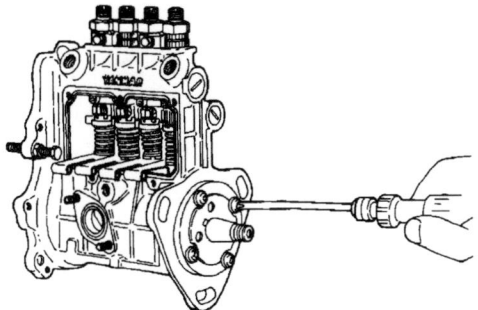

NOTE: Coat the camshaft and oil seal with oil to prevent the oil seal from being scratched.

(14) Fix the pump, lightly tap both ends of the cam shaft with a wood hammer, and adjust the cam shaft side clearance with the adjustment shims while checking with side clearance gauge.

	mm (in.)
Camshaft side clearance	0.02 ~ 0.05 (0.0007 ~ 0.0019)

Adjusting
Pull out adjusting shims if clearance is too small, and add adjusting shims if it is too large.

	mm (in.)
Adjusting shim thickness	0.50 (0.0196) 0.40 (0.0157) 0.30 (0.0118) 0.15 (0.0059)

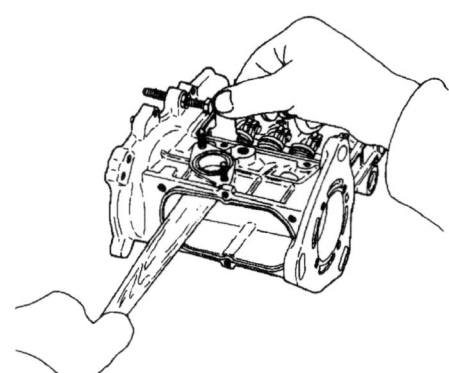

(15) Mount the fuel pump side cover.
(16) Tap in the camshaft wood ruff key.
(17) Turn the camshaft, and pull out the plunger spring support plate.

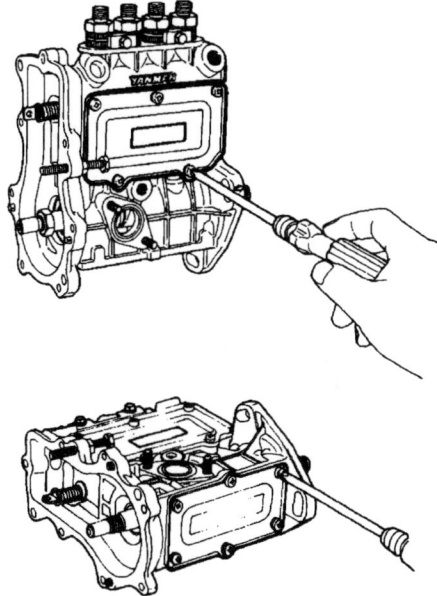

NOTE: Fit double nuts to turn the camshaft.

Chapter 3 Fuel Injection Equipment
3. Disassembly, Reassembly and Inspection of Fuel Injection Pump — 4JH Series

(18) Tighten delivery valve retainer.

(20) Mount the fuel feed pump

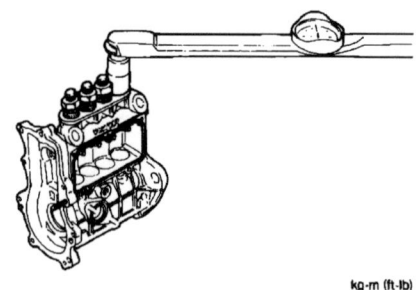
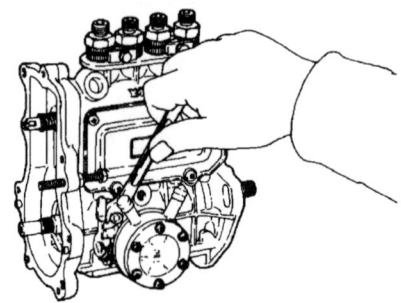

Tightening torque	kg-m (ft-lb)
	3.5 ~ 4.0 (25.31 ~ 28.93)

NOTE: 1. Tighten the retainer as far as possible by hand— if the bolt gets hard to turn part way, the packing or delivery valve are out of place. Remove, correct, and start tightening again.
2. Overtightening can result in malfunctioning of the rack.

NOTE: See the item explaining reassembly of the fuel feed pump.

(19) Fit the delivery retainer stop and tighten the stop bolt.

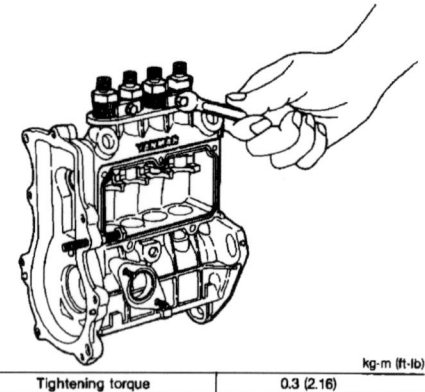

Tightening torque	kg-m (ft-lb)
	0.3 (2.16)

NOTE: Overtightening can upset the delivery retainer and cause oil leakage.

4. Adjustment of Fuel Injection Pump and Governor

Adjust the fuel injection pump after you have completed reassembly. The pump itself must be readjusted with a special pump tester when you have replaced major parts such as the plunger assembly, roller guide assembly, fuel camshaft, etc. Procure a pump tester like the one illustrated below.

4-1 Preparations

Prepare for adjustment of the fuel injection pump as follows:

(1) Adjusting nozzle assembly and inspection of injection starting pressure.

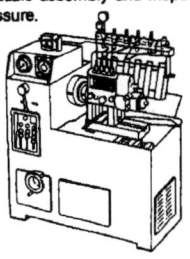

Adjusting nozzle type	YDN-12SD12
Injection starting pressure	165 ~ 175 (2346.85 ~ 2489.08)

kg/cm² (lb/in.²)

(2) Adjusting injection pipe.

mm (in.)

Inner dia./outer dia. × length	2.0/6.0 × 600 (0.0787/0.2362 × 23.6220)
Minimum bending radius	25 (0.9842)

(3) Mount the fuel injection pump on the pump tester platform.

mm (in.)

Tester used	l_1	l_2	Part code number
Yanmar	110 (4.3307)	150 (5.9055)	158090-51010
Robert Bosch	125 (4.9212)	165 (6.4960)	158090-51020

(4) Remove the control rack blind cover and fit the rack indicator.

Next, turn the pinion from the side of the pump until the control rack is at the maximum drive side position, and set it to the rack indicator scale standard position. Then make sure that the control rack and rack indicator slide smoothly.

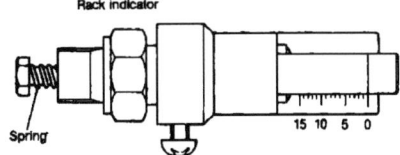

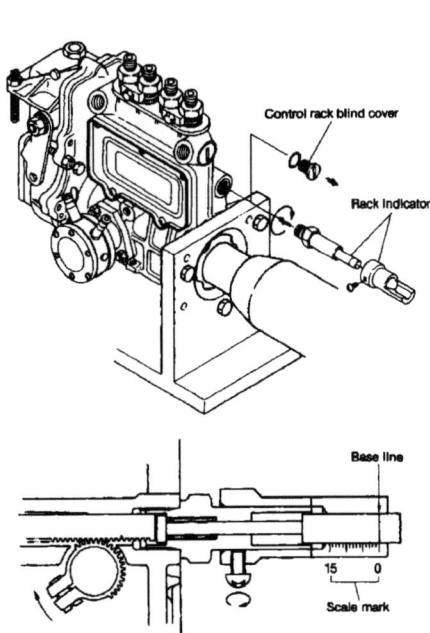

Part code number	158090-51500

Chapter 3 Fuel Injection Equipment
4. Adjustment of Fuel Injection Pump and Governor

4JH Series

(5) Check control rack stroke
Make sure the rack position is at 11.5 ~ 12.5mm (0.4527 ~ 0.4921in.) on the indicator scale when the governor control lever is set at the maximum operating position. If it is not at this value, change the link connecting the governor and control rack to adjust it.

NOTE: *Links are availabe in 1mm (0.0394in.) increments.*

(6) Remove the plug in the oil fill hole on the top of the governor case, and fill the pump with about 200cc of pump oil or engine oil.

Relation between top clearance, standard shim thickness and pre-stroke.

mm (in.)

Adjusting shim thickness	1.0 (0.0394)
	1.2 (0.0472)
	1.3 (0.0512)
	1.4 (0.0551)
	1.5 (0.0591)
	1.6 (0.0630)
Part Code No.	129155–51600

(1) Place the top clearance gauge on a level surface and set the gauge to zero.

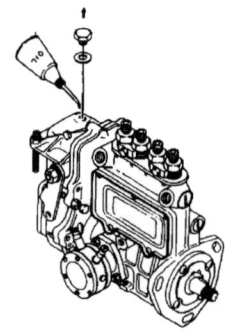

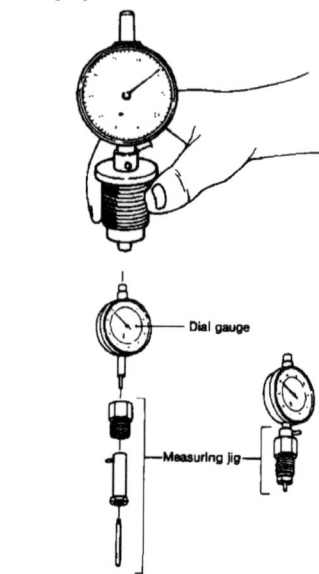

(7) Complete fuel oil piping and operate the pump tester to purge the line of air.
(8) Set the pressure of oil fed from pump tester to injection pump at 0.2 ~ 0.3kg/cm² (2.84 ~ 4.26 lb/in.²).

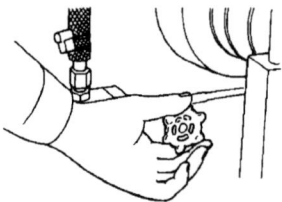

(2) Remove the injection pump delivery retainer, take out the delivery valve assembly, insert the top clearance gauge and tighten by hand.

4-2 Adjustment of top clearance

Adjust the top clearance (clearance between top of plunger and top of barrel with cam at top dead point) of each cylinder plunger to bring it to the specified value by changing the thickness of the shims.

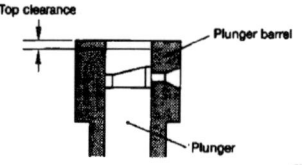

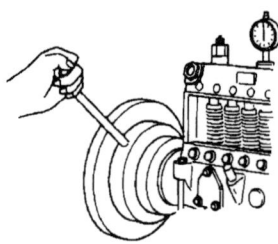

(3) Turn the camshaft, and bring cam to top dead point while watching gauge needle.

mm (in.)

Top clearance	0.95–1.05 (0.0374–0.0413)
Pre-stroke	2.5 (0.0984)
Standard shim thickness	1.2 (0.0472)

Chapter 3 Fuel Injection Equipment
4. Adjustment of Fuel Injection Pump and Governor

4JH Series

(4) Read the gauge at this position, and adjust until the clearance is at the specified value by changing adjusting shims.
Tighten the adjusting screw after completing adjustment.

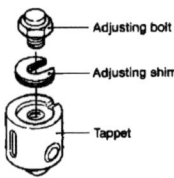

(Greater shim thickness decreases top clearance and smaller shim thickness increases top clearance).

NOTE: Adjust while watching gauge, and then tighten.

(5) After adjustment is completed, insert the delivery valve assembly and tighten the delivery retainer.

kg-m (ft-lb)

Delivery retainer tightening torque	3.5 ~ 4.0 (25.31 ~ 28.93)

Repeat the above procedure to adjust the top clearance of each cylinder.

4-3 Adjusting of injection timing

After adjusting the top clearance for all cylinders, check/adjust the injection timing.

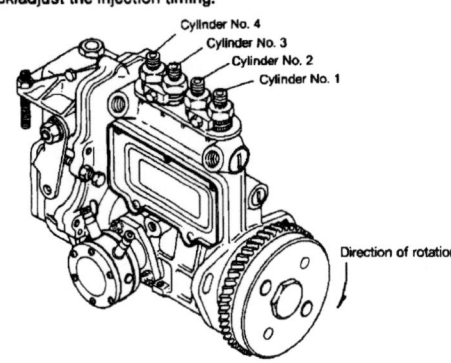

(1) Set the governor control lever to the operating position and fix (bring plunger to the effective injection range), turn the camshaft clockwise, and check the injection starting time (FID) of cylinder No.1 (start of discharge of fuel from the delivery retainer).

Cylinder no.	Count from the drive side
Direction of rotation	Right looking from drive side

(2) In the above state, set the tester needle to a position easy to read on the flywheel scale, and check the injection timing several times by reading the flywheel scale, according to the injection order.

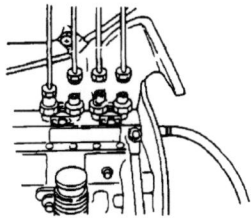

Injection order	1—3—4—2—1
Injection timing	90°
Allowable deviation	±30'

(3) Readjust the top clearance of cylinders that are not within the allowable deviation (increasing adjusting shim thickness makes injection timing faster, and decreasing makes it slower).
The change in injection timing effected by adjusting shims is as follows:

Change in shim thickness	Change in injection timing	
	Cam angle	Crank angle
0.1mm (0.0039in.)	0.5°	1.0°

(4) When you have readjusted top clearance, make sure it is within allowable values after completing adjustment.

mm (in.)

Allowable top clearance	0.3 (0.0118)

NOTE: 1. All cylinders must be readjusted if one shows less than the allowable value.
2. If the top clearance is less than the allowable value, the plunger will hit the delivery valve or the plunger flange will hit the plunger barrel.

Chapter 3 Fuel Injection Equipment
4. Adjustment of Fuel Injection Pump and Governor

4-4 Plunger pressure test

(1) Mount the pressure gauge to the delivery retainer of the cylinder to be tested.

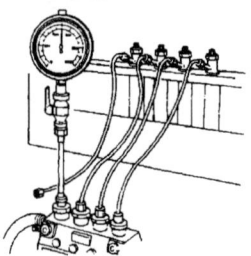

Max. pressure gauge reading	1000 kg/cm² (14223 lb/in.²)
Connecting screw dimensions	M12 × 1.5

(2) Set the governor control lever to the stop position, operate the injection pump at about 200 rpm, and make sure that the pressure gauge reading is 500 kg/cm² (7110 lb/in.²) or more while lightly moving the control pinion gear towards full throttle (drive side) from the pump.
Replace the plunger if the pressure does not reach this value.
(3) Immediately release the gear after pressure rises to stop injection.
At the same time, check to see that oil is not leaking from the delivery retainer or fuel injection piping, and that there is no extreme drop in pressure.

4-5 Delivery valve pressure test

(1) Perform the plunger pressure test in the same way, bringing the pressure to about 120 kg/cm² (1706 lb/in.²), and then stopping injection.

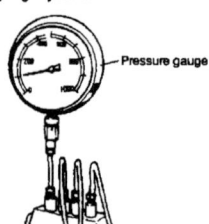
Pressure gauge

(2) After pressure rises to the above value, measure the time it takes to drop from 100 ~ 90 kg/cm² (1422 ~ 2702 lb/in.²).

100 → 90 kg/cm² (1422 ~ 1280 lb/in.²)	5 seconds (to drop 10 kg/cm² (142 lb/in.²))

If the pressure drops faster than this, wash the delivery valve, and retest. Replace the delivery valve if the pressure continues to drop rapidly.

4-6 Adjusting injection volume (uniformity of each cylinder)

The injection volume is determined by the fuel injection pump rpm and rack position. Check and adjust to bring to specified value.

4-6.1 Measuring injection volume

(1) Preparation
Set the pump rpm, rack position and measuring stroke to the specified value and measure:

Pump RPM	1800 rpm
Pump rotating direction	Right looking from drive side
Rack indicator scale reading	7mm (0.2756 in)

Remove the rack stop bolt behind the pump and screw in the rack fixing bolt to fix rack.

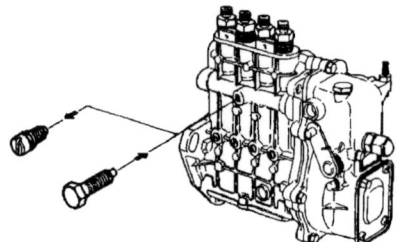

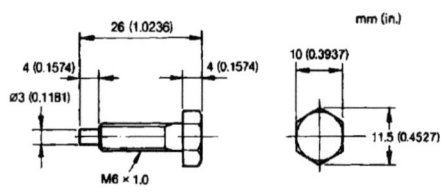

Part Code No.	158090-51510

(2) Measuring injection volume
Measure the injection volume at the standard stroke, and adjust as follows if it is not within the specified value.

Measuring stroke	1,000 st
Specified injection volume at standard rack position	See injection pump service data
Nonuniformity of cylinders	±3%

4-6.2 Adjustment of injection volume

Compare the injection volume collected in measuring cylinders for each cylinder, and adjust if necessary to obtain specified value.
(1) Push the control rack all the way to the drive side, stop with rack fixing bolt, and loosen the pinion/sleeve fixing bolt 1/3 revolution.

Chapter 3 Fuel Injection Equipment
4. Adjustment of Fuel Injection Pump and Governor ──────────── 4JH Series

(2) When the control sleeve is turned to the right or left, the plunger is turned through the same angle to increase or decrease injection volume.
The injection volume is increased when the control sleeve is turned in the direction of the → and is decreased when turned in the direction of the ← on the following figure.

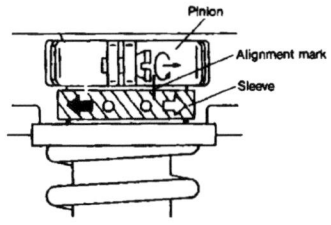

(3) Measure the injection volume of each cylinder again. Repeat this process until the injection volume for every cylinder is the same (within specified limit).
(4) Next, measure the injection volumes under different conditions, and make sure the injection volume for every cylinder is within specifications.
Replace the plunger if the injection volume is not within specifications.

NOTE: *See adjustment data for the specified injection volume value at other measuring points.*

(5) After completing measurement, firmly tighten the piston/sleeve fixing screw.
(6) If not aligned with match mark, make a new match mark.

4-7 Adjustment of governor

4-7.1 Adjusting fuel limit bolt

(1) Adjust the tightness of the fuel limit bolt to bring the rack position to the specified value (R_1) with the governor control lever all the way down towards the fuel increase position, while keeping the pump at rated rpm N_1.

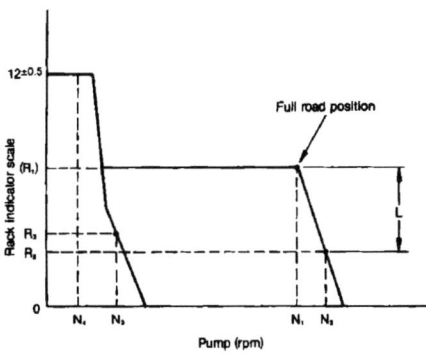

(2) Measure fuel injection volume at rack position (R_1). Tightening of fuel limit bolt.
(3) If the injection volume is at the specified value, tighten the fuel limit bolt lock nut at that position.

4-7.2 Adjusting RPM limit bolt

(1) Gradually loosen the governor control lever while keeping the pump drive condition in the same condition as when the fuel limit bolt was adjusted, and adjust the tightness of the RPM limit bolt to the point where the rack position just exceeds the specified value (R_1).

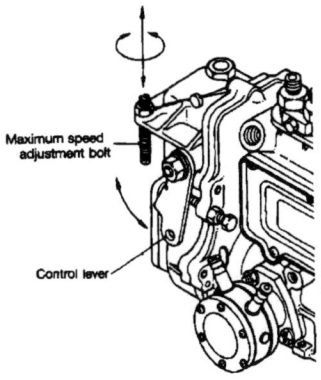

(2) Check maximum RPM at no load
Further increase rpm, and make sure that rack position ($R_2 = R_1 - L$) corresponding to maximum rpm at no load is within specified value (N_2).

No load max. RPM (Pump RPM)	1950 rpm

4-7.3 Adjusting idling

(1) Maintain the pump rpm at specified rpm (N_3).

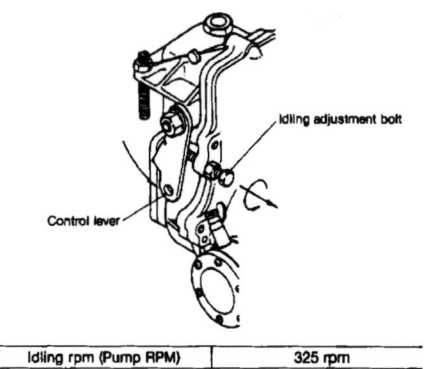

Idling rpm (Pump RPM)	325 rpm

Chapter 3 Fuel Injection Equipment
4. Adjustment of Fuel Injection Pump and Governor

4JH Series

(2) Measure the injection volume while lowering the governor control lever to the idling position, and adjust the position of the control lever with the idling adjustment bolt to bring it to specified value.

Measuring stroke	1000 st
Idling injection volume	See injection pump service data

4-7.4 Check injection volume when starting

(1) Make sure the control rack moves smoothly while gradually reducing idling rpm.
(2) Next, fix the governor control lever at full load position with the pump at specified rpm (N_4). Make sure that control rack is at maximum rack position (11.05 ~ 12.05).
Measure the injection volume and check to make sure it is within the specified value.

Pump rpm (N^4)	200 rpm
Rack indicator scale	11.5~12.5mm(0.4527~0.4921 in.)
Measuring stroke	1000 st
Injection volume	See injection pump service data

Check injection stop
Drive the pump at rated rpm (N_1) and standard rack position (R_1) with governor control lever at full load position, operate the stop lever on the back of the governor case, and make sure that injection to all cylinders is stopped.

NOTE: Be sure to remove the rack fixing bolt when doing this.

5. Automatic Timer (Automatic Advancing Timer)

5-1 Timer construction

The faster the engine rpm, the larger the crank angle is during ignition delay. This results in a delay in ignition time and thus a decrease in engine output.

When an engine is used from low to high rpm, the injection timing must be changed according to engine rpm to maintain it at the optimum timing.

The automatic timer uses centrifugal force to automatically adjust injection timing.

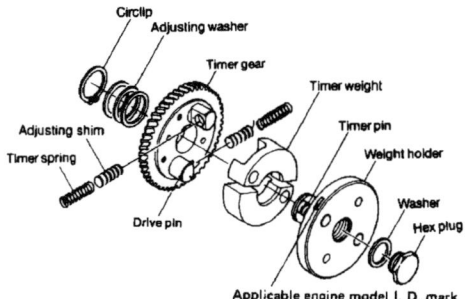

Applicable engine model I. D. mark

		I. D. Mark	Applicable Engine Model & E/#		Advanced angle
Automatic Timer Ass'y (Automatic Advancing Timer)	Old type	JH-A0	4JHE	E/# 00101 ~ 00574	7°
		JH-A1	4JHE	E/# 01000 and before	5.5°
		JH-B0	4JH-TE	E/# 11000 and before	3.5°
		JH-C0	4JH-HTE	E/# 21000 and before	2.5°
	New type	TN-A0	4JHE	E/# 01001 and after	4°
		JH-C0	4JH-TE	E/# 11001 and after	2.5°
			4JH-HTE	E/# 21001 and after	
			4JH-DTE	E/# 30101 and after	

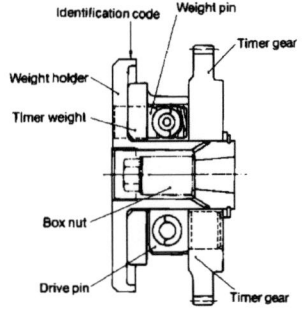
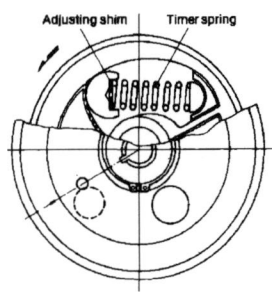

Chapter 3 Fuel Injection Equipment
5. Automatic Advancing Timer

4JH Series

5-2 Functioning and characteristics of timer

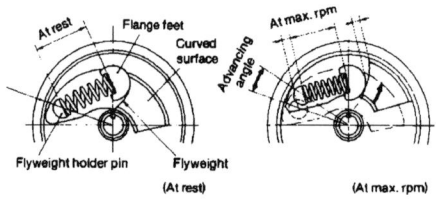

Flyweight holder pin   Flyweight
(At rest)   (At max. rpm)

The spring is pressed against the center of the flyweight. As rpm increases, the centrifugal force of the two flyweights increases, compresses the timer spring, and the position of the weight holder and flange changes due to the movement of the curved surface of the weight, changing the injection timing. Accordingly, as the spring is compressed (according to the rise in rpm advancing the timing), the advancing angle remains proportional to rpm.

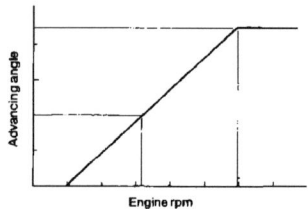

Engine rpm

The advancing characteristics can be changed by changing the profile of the side of the weight and the spring constant of the spring.

5-3 Timer disassembly

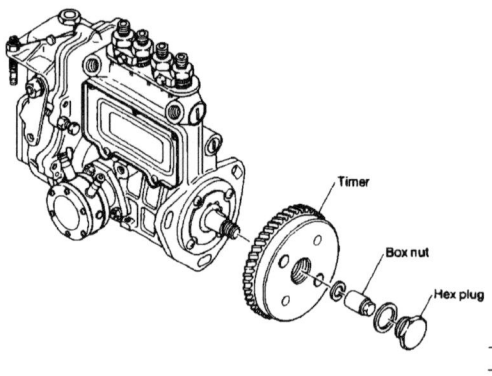

(1) Remove the hex plugs from both ends of timer.
(2) Use a box spanner to remove the cam shaft box nut.
(3) Use a gear pulling tool to remove the timer assembly.
(4) The spring, shim and weight can be removed when you take off the gear circlip and separate the timer and weight holder.

NOTE: *As the advancing angle has been set at the factory, do not disassemble the timer unless necessary.*

5-4 Timer Inspection

(1) Inspect the timer ring, and replace if there is excessive settling or corrosion.
(2) Inspect the curved surface of the timer weight and the portion of drive pin it comes in contact with, and replace if wear is excessive or movement is not smooth.

NOTE: *1. Recheck advancing angle when replacing weight or spring, and readjust as necessary with adjusting shims.*
2. If you change weight holders, measure the shaft side clearance, and adjust with washers.

mm (in.)

Standard side clearance	0.02 ~ 0.10 (0.0007 ~ 0.0039)

5-5 Timer reassembly

(1) Mount the timer assembly on the fuel injection pump camshaft, and tighten the box nut with a box spanner.

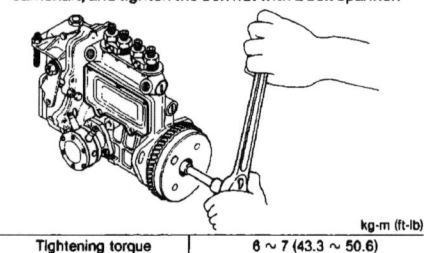

kg-m (ft-lb)

Tightening torque	6 ~ 7 (43.3 ~ 50.6)

NOTE: *The box nut is tightened by turning it right looking from the drive side.*

(2) Apply grease around the box nut, and tighten the hex plug.

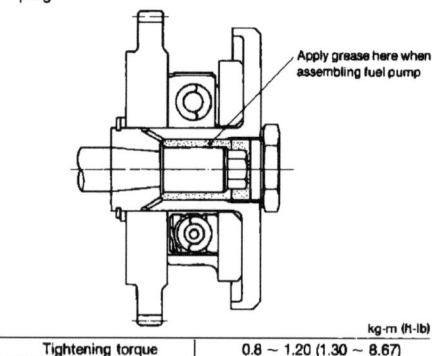

Apply grease here when assembling fuel pump

kg-m (ft-lb)

Tightening torque	0.8 ~ 1.20 (1.30 ~ 8.67)

Chapter 3 Fuel Injection Equipment
6. Fuel Feed Pump

4JH Series

6. Fuel Feed Pump

The fuel feed pump pumps fuel from the fuel tank, passes it through the fuel filter element, and supplies it to the fuel injection pump.
The fuel feed pump is mounted on the side of this engine and is driven by the (eccentric) cam of the fuel pump camshaft. It is provided with a manual priming lever so that fuel can be supplied when the engine is stopped.

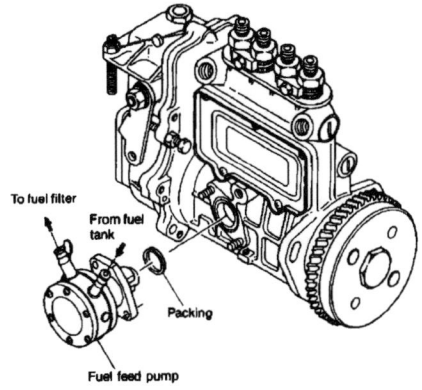

6-1 Construction of fuel feed pump

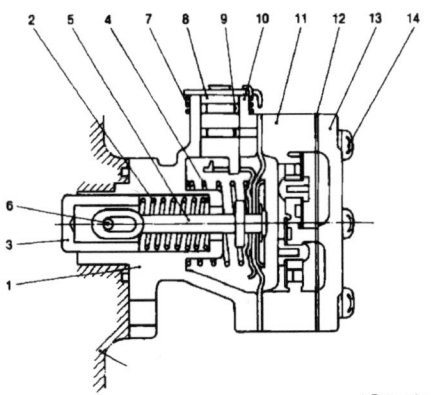

1. Bottom body
2. Piston spring
3. Piston
4. Diaphragm spring
5. Diaphragm assembly
6. Pin
7. Lever return spring
8. Lever assembly
9. O-ring
10. Stop pin
11. Top body assembly
12. Packing
13. Cover
14. Small screw
15. Cap

6-2 Fuel feed pump specifications

Head	1m (3.28 ft)
Discharge volume	230 cc/min (14.03 in.³/min) at 1500 cam rpm, discharge pressure of 0.2 kg/cm² (2.84 lb/in.²)
Closed off pressure	0.3 kg/cm² (4.26 lb/in.²) or more (at 400 cam rpm)

Chapter 3 Fuel Injection Equipment
6. Fuel Feed Pump

6-3 Disassembly and reassembly of fuel feed pump

6-3.1 Disassembly

(1) Remove the fuel feed pump mounting nut, and take the fuel feed pump off the fuel injection pump.
(2) Clean the fuel feed pump assembly with fuel oil.
(3) After checking the orientation of the arrow on the cover, make match marks on the upper body and cover, remove the small screw, and disassemble the cover, upper body and lower body.

6-3.2 Reassembly

(1) Clean all parts with fuel oil, inspect, and replace any defective parts.
(2) Replace any packings on parts that have been disassembled.
(3) Make sure that the intake valve and discharge valve on upper body are mounted in the proper direction, and that you don't forget the valve packing.
(4) Assemble the diaphragm into the body, making sure the diaphragm mounting holes are lined up (do not force).
(5) Align the match marks on the upper body of the pump and cover, and tighten the small screws evenly.

	kg-cm (ft-lb)
Tightening torque	15 ~ 25 (1.08 ~ 1.80)

(4) Valve contact/mounting
Clean the valve seat and valve with air to remove any foreign matter.

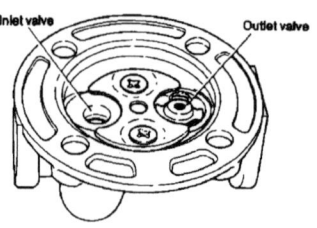

(5) Inspect the diaphragm spring and piston spring for settling and the piston for wear, and replace as necessary.

NOTE: Replace parts as an assembly.

6-4 Fuel feed pump inspection

(1) Place the fuel feed pump in kerosene, cover the discharge port with your finger, move the priming lever and check for air bubbles (Repair or replace any part which emits air bubbles).

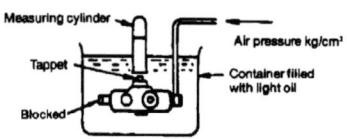

(2) Attach a vinyl hose to the fuel feed pump intake, keep the pump at the specified depth from the fuel oil surface, move the priming lever by hand and check for sudden spurts of fuel oil from the discharge port. If oil is not spurted out, inspect the diaphragm and diaphragm spring and repair/replace as necessary.

(3) Diaphragm inspection
Parts of the diaphragm that are repeatedly burned will become thinner or deteriorate over a long period of time. Check diaphragm and replace if necessary.

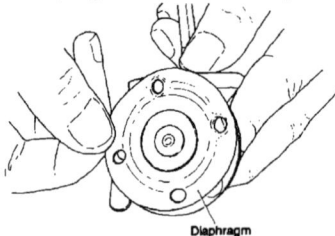

7. Fuel Injection Nozzle

When fuel oil pumped by the fuel injection pump reaches the injection nozzle, it pushes up the nozzle valve (held down by spring), and is injected into the combustion chamber at high pressure.

The fuel is atomized by the nozzle to mix uniformly with the air in the combustion chamber. How well the fuel is mixed with high temperature air directly affects combustion efficiency, engine performance and fuel economy.

Accordingly, the fuel injection nozzles must be kept in top-condition to maintain performance and operating efficiency.

7-1 Functioning of fuel injection nozzle

Fuel from the fuel injection pump passes through the oil port in the nozzle holder, and enters the nozzle body reservoir.

When oil reaches the specified pressure, it pushes up the nozzle valve (held by the nozzle spring), and is injected through the small hole on the tip of the nozzle body.

The nozzle valve is automatically pushed down by the nozzle spring and closed after fuel is injected.

Oil that leaks from between the nozzle valve and nozzle body goes from the hole on top of the nozzle spring through the oil leakage fitting and back into the fuel tank.

Adjustment of injection starting pressure is effected with the adjusting shims.

(1) Hole type fuel injection nozzle

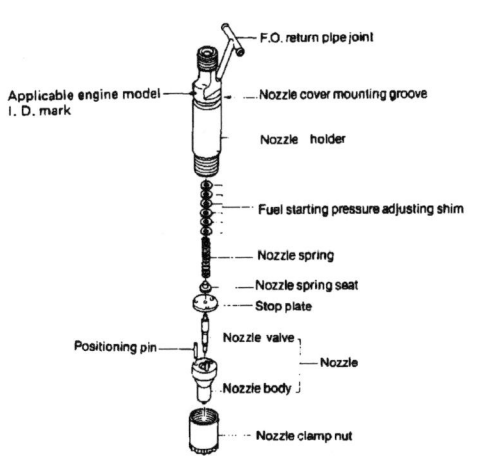
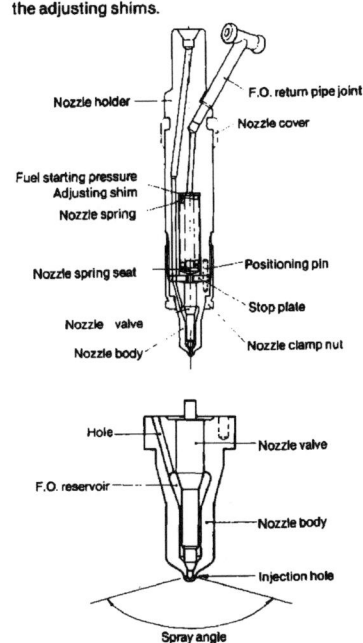

Fuel Injection Nozzle Ass'y I. D. Mark	A	E	B	D	F	G		
Spray angle	150°	155°	150°	145°	155°	140°		
Nozzle opening pressure			195 ~ 205 kg/cm² (2,773 ~ 2,915 lb/in.²)					
No. of injection hole x dia	4 x 0.24mm (0.0094 in.)		4 x 0.28mm (0.0110 in.)	5 x 0.26mm (0.0102 in.)	4 x 0.24mm (0.0094 in.)	5 x 0.25mm (0.0098 in.)		
Nozzle I. D. mark	150P244J0	155P244J1	150P284J0	145P265J1	155P265J1	140P255J2		
Applicable engine model	4JHE			4JH-TE	4JH-HTE	4JHE	4JH-TE	4JH-HTE	4JH-DTE
Applicable engine No.	#00101 ~ 00574	#00575 ~ 01000	#00101 ~ 11000	#20101 ~ 21000	#01001 and after	#11001 and after	#21001 and after	#30101 and after

Chapter 3 Fuel Injection Equipment
7. Fuel Injection Nozzle

4JH Series

(3) Nozzle body identification number
The type of nozzle can be determined from the number inscribed on the outside of the nozzle body.
1) Hole type fuel injection nozzles

Sample

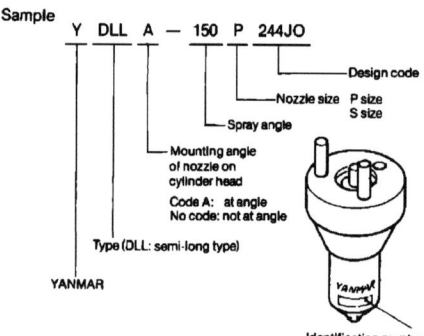

Y DLL A — 150 P 244JO
- Design code
- Nozzle size P size / S size
- Spray angle
- Mounting angle of nozzle on cylinder head
  Code A: at angle
  No code: not at angle
- Type (DLL: semi-long type)
- YANMAR

Identification number

7-3 Fuel injection nozzle disassembly

NOTE: 1. Disassemble fuel injection nozzle in a clean area as for fuel injection pump.
2. When disassembling more than one fuel injection nozzle, keep the parts for each injection nozzle separate for each cylinder (i.e. the nozzle for cylinder 1 must be remounted in cylinder 1).

(1) When removing the injection nozzle from the cylinder head, remove the high pressure fuel pipe, fuel leakage pipe, etc., the injection nozzle retainer nut, and then the fuel injection nozzle.

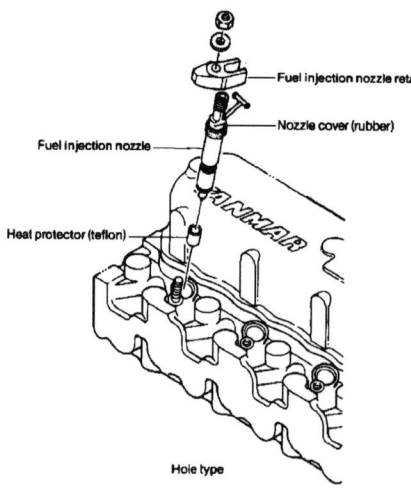

- Fuel injection nozzle retainer
- Nozzle cover (rubber)
- Fuel injection nozzle
- Heat protector (teflon)

Hole type

(2) Put the nozzle in a vise
NOTE: Use the special nozzle holder for the hole type injection nozzle so that the high pressure mounting threads are not damaged.
(3) Remove the nozzle nut

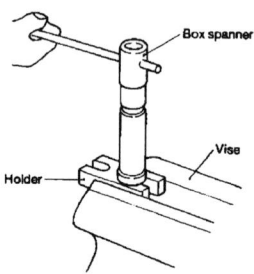

- Box spanner
- Vise
- Holder

NOTE: Use a special box spanner for the hole type (the thickness of the two nozzle nuts is 15mm (0.5906in.)).

(4) Remove the inner parts
NOTE: Be careful not to loosen the spring seat, adjusting shims or other small parts.

7-4 Fuel injection nozzle inspection
7-4.1 Washing
(1) Make sure to use new diesel oil to wash the fuel injection nozzle parts.
(2) Wash the nozzle in clean diesel oil with the nozzle cleaning kit.

Nozzle cleaning kit

1) Diesel Kiki nozzle cleaning kit:
   Type NP-8486B No. 5789-001
2) Anzen Jidosha Co., Ltd. nozzle cleaning kit:
   Type NCK-001

(3) Clean off the carbon on the outside of the nozzle body with a brass brush.

(4) Clean the nozzle seat with cleaning spray.

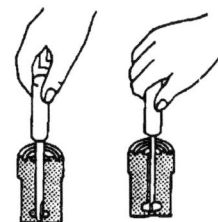

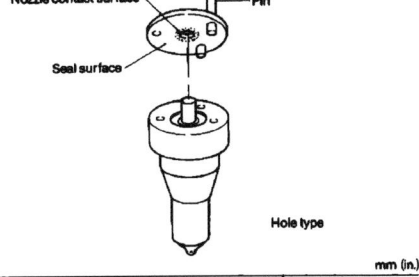

	mm (in.)
Nozzle contact surface wear limit	0.1 (0.0039)

(5) Clean off the carbon on the tip of nozzle with a piece of wood.
(6) Clean hole type nozzles with a nozzle cleaning needle.

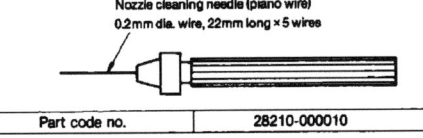

Nozzle cleaning needle (piano wire)
0.2mm dia. wire, 22mm long × 5 wires

Part code no.	28210-000010

(4) Inspecting nozzle spring
Replace the nozzle spring if it is extremely bent, or the surface is scratched or rusted.

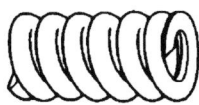

7-4.2 Nozzle Inspection

(1) Inspect for scratches/wear
Inspect oil seals for abnormal scratches or wear and replace nozzle if the nozzle sliding surface or seat are scratched or abnormally worn.

(2) Check nozzle sliding
Wash the nozzle and nozzle body in clean diesel oil, and make sure that when the nozzle is pulled out about half way from the body, it slides down by itself when released.
Rotate the nozzle a little; replace nozzle/nozzle body as a set if there are some places where it does not slide smoothly.

(5) Nozzle holder
Check oil seal surface for scratches/wear; replace if wear is excessive.

7-5 Fuel injection nozzle reassembly

The fuel injection nozzle is reassembled in the opposite order to disassembly.
(1) Insert the adjusting shims, nozzle spring and nozzle spring seat in the nozzle holder, mount the stop plate with the pin, insert the nozzle body/nozzle set and tighten the nut.
(2) Use the special holder when tightening the nut for the hole type nozzle as in disassembly.

Nozzle nut tightening torque	kg-m (ft-lb)
Hole type nozzle	4 ~ 4.5 (28.9 ~ 32.5)

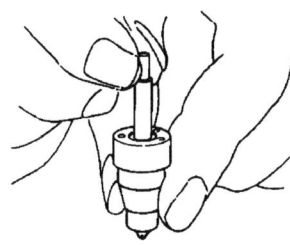

(3) Inspecting stop plate (inter-piece)
Check for scratches/wear in seals on both ends, check for abnormal wear on the surface where it comes in contact with the nozzle; replace if stop plate is excessively worn.

Chapter 3 Fuel Injection Equipment
7. Fuel Injection Nozzle

4JH Series

7-6 Adjusting fuel injection nozzle

7-6.1 Adjusting opening pressure

Mount the fuel injection nozzle on the nozzle tester and use the handle to measure injection starting pressure. If it is not at specified pressure, use the adjusting shims to increase/decrease pressure (both hole and pintle types).

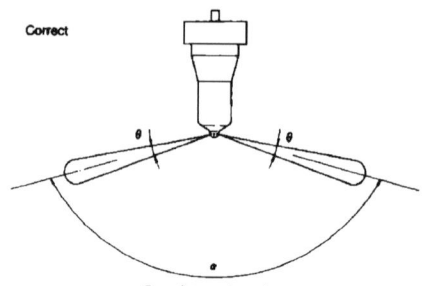

Correct

Spray from each nozzle hole is uniform

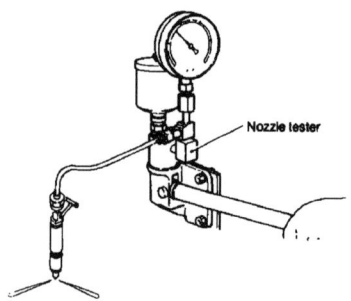

Nozzle tester

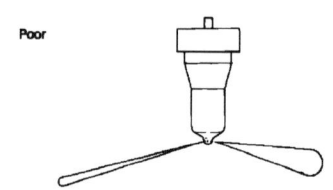

Poor

- Excessive difference in spray angle (θ)
- Excessive difference in injection angle (α)
- Incomplete atomization
- Sluggish starting/stopping of injection

Injection starting pressure

Injection starting pressure	kg/cm² (lb/in.²)
	195 ~ 205 (2773 ~ 2915)

7-6.2 Injection test

After adjusting the nozzle to the specified starting pressure, check the fuel spray condition and seat oil tightness.

(1) Check seat oil tightness

After two or three injections, gradually increase the pressure up to 20 kg/cm² (284 lb/in.²) before reading the starting pressure, maintain the pressure for 5 seconds, and make sure that no oil is dripping from the tip of the nozzle.

Test the injection with a nozzle tester; retighten and test again if there is excessive oil leakage from the overflow coupling.

Replace the nozzle as a set if oil leakage is still excessive.

(2) Injection spray condition

Operate the nozzle tester lever once to twice a second and check for abnormal injection.

1) Hole type nozzles

Replace hole type nozzles that do not satisfy the following conditions:
- Proper spray angle (θ)
- Correct injection angle (α)
- Complete atomization of fuel
- Prompt starting/stopping of injection

Chapter 3 Fuel Injection Equipment
8. Troubleshooting

4JH Series

8. Troubleshooting

1. Troubleshooting of fuel injection pump

Complete repair means not only replacing defective parts, but finding and eliminating the cause of the trouble as well. The cause of the trouble may not necessarily be in the pump itself, but may be in the engine or the fuel system. If the pump is removed prematurely, the true cause of the trouble may never be known. Before removing the pump from the engine, at least go through the basic check points given here.

Basic check points
- Check for breaks or oil leaks throughout the fuel system, from the fuel tank to the nozzle.
- Check the injection timings for all cylinders. Are they correctly adjusted? Are they too fast or too slow?
- Check the nozzle spray.
- Check the fuel delivery. Is it in good condition? Loosen the fuel pipe connection at the injection pump inlet, and test operate the fuel feed pump.

2. Major faults and troubleshooting

Fault		Cause	Remedy
1. Engine won't start.	Fuel not delivered to injection pump.	(1) No fuel in the fuel tank.	Resupply
		(2) Fuel tank cock is closed.	Open
		(3) Fuel pipe system is clogged.	Clean
		(4) Fuel filter element is clogged.	Disassemble and clean, or replace element
		(5) Air is sucked into the fuel due to defective connections in the piping from the fuel tank to the fuel pump.	Repair
		(6) Defective valve contact of feed pump	Repair or replace.
		(7) Piston spring of feed pump is broken.	Replace
		(8) Inter-spindle or tappets of feed pump are stuck.	Repair or replace
	Fuel delivered to injection pump.	(1) Defective connection of control lever and accel. rod of injection pump.	Repair or adjust
		(2) Plunger is worn out or stuck.	Repair or replace
		(3) Delivery valve is stuck.	Repair or replace
		(4) Control rack doesn't move.	Repair or replace
		(5) Injection pump coupling is damaged, or the key is broken.	Replace
	Nozzle doesn't work.	(1) Nozzle valve doesn't open or close normally.	Repair or replace
		(2) Nozzle seat is defective.	Repair or replace
		(3) Case nut is loose.	Inspect and tighten
		(4) Injection nozzle starting pressure is too low.	Adjust
		(5) Nozzle spring is broken.	Replace
		(6) Fuel oil filter is clogged.	Repair or replace
		(7) Excessive oil leaks from the nozzle sliding area.	Replace the nozzle assembly
	Injection timing is defective.	(1) Injection timing is retarded due to failure of the coupling.	Adjust
		(2) Camshaft is excessively worn.	Replace camshaft
		(3) Roller guide incorrectly adjusted or excessively worn.	Adjust or replace
		(4) Plunger is excessively worn.	Replace plunger assembly
2. Engine starts, but immediately stops.		(1) Fuel pipe is clogged.	Clean
		(2) Fuel filter is clogged.	Disassemble and clean, or replace the element.
		(3) Improper air-tightness of the fuel pipe connection, or pipe is broken and air is being sucked in.	Replace packing; repair pipe
		(4) Insufficient fuel delivery from the feed pump.	Repair or replace

Chapter 3 Fuel Injection Equipment
8. Troubleshooting
4JH Series

Fault		Cause	Remedy
3. Engine's output is insufficient.	Defective injection timing, and other failures.	(1) Knocking sounds caused by improper (too fast) injection timing. (2) Engine overheats or emits large amount of smoke due to improper (too slow) injection timing. (3) Insufficient fuel delivery from feed pump.	Inspect and adjust Inspect and adjust Repair or replace
	Nozzle movements is defective	(1) Case nut loose. (2) Defective injection nozzle performance. (3) Nozzle spring is broken. (4) Excessive oil leaks from nozzle.	Inspect and retighten Repair or replace nozzle Replace Replace nozzle assembly
	Injection pump is defective.	(1) Max. delivery limit bolt is screwed in too far. (2) Plunger is worn. (3) Injection amount is not uniform. (4) Injection timings are not even. (5) The 1st and 2nd levers of the governor and the control rack of the injection pump are improperly lined up. (6) Delivery stopper is loose. (7) Delivery packing is defective. (8) Delivery valve seat is defective. (9) Delivery spring is broken.	Adjust Replace Adjust Adjust Repair Inspect and retighten Replace packing Repair or replace Replace

4. Idling is rough.		(1) Movement of control rack is defective.
		  1) Stiff plunger movement or sticking.
		  2) Rack and pinion fitting is defective.
		  3) Movement of governor is improper.
		  4) Delivery stopper is too tight.
		(2) Uneven injection volume.
		(3) Injection timing is defective.
		(4) Plunger is worn and fuel injection adjustment is difficult.
		(5) Governor spring is too weak.
		(6) Feed pump can't feed oil at low speeds.
		(7) Fuel supply is insufficient at low speeds due to clogging of fuel filter.
			
			Repair or replace
			Repair
			Repair
			Inspect and adjust
			Adjust
			Adjust
			Replace
			Replace
			Repair or replace
			Disassemble and clean, or replace element

5. Engine runs at high speeds, but cuts out at low speeds.		(1) The wire or rod of the accel. is caught. (2) Control rack is caught and can't be moved.	Inspect and repair Inspect and repair
6. Engine doesn't reach max. rpm.		(1) Governor spring is broken or excessively worn. (2) Injection performance of nozzle is poor.	Replace Repair or replace
7. Loud knocking.		(1) Injection timing is too fast or too slow. (2) Injection from nozzle is improper. Fuel drips after each injection. (3) Injection nozzle starting pressure is too high. (4) Uneven injection. (5) Engine overheats, or insufficient compression.	Adjust Adjust Adjust Adjust Repair
8. Engine exhausts too much smoke.	When exhaust smoke is black:	(1) Injection timing is too fast. (2) Air volume intake is insufficient. (3) The amount of injection is uneven. (4) Injection from nozzle is improper.	Adjust Inspect and repair Adjust Repair or replace
	When exhaust smoke is white:	(1) Injection timing is too slow. (2) Water is mixed in fuel. (3) Shortage of lube oil in the engine. (4) Engine is over-cooled.	Adjust Inspect fuel system, and clean Repair Inspect

Chapter 3 Fuel Injection Equipment
9. Fuel Injection Pump Service Data

July 18 '85

Adjustment	Item		4JHE			4JH-TE			4JH-HTE			4JH-UTE		
	Engine model	Part No.	729470 – 51300			729472 – 51300			729474 – 51300			729473 – 51300		
	Assemble code		B300			B303			B306			B364		
		I.D. mark												
	Adjustment specs.		Engine specs.		Calibration specs.	Engine specs.		Calibration specs.	Engine specs.		Calibration specs.	Engine specs.		Calibration specs.
4-1-(1)	Nozzle type	I.D.mark	150P24AUO/**155P24AIJ		DN-12SD12	150P28AUO/**140P26SI2		DN-12SD12	146P26SI1/**140P26SI2		DN-12SD12	140P26SI2		DN-12SD12
	Injection starting pressure	kg/cm² (lb/in²)	195 ~ 205 (2,773 ~ 2,915)		165 ~ 175 (2,346 ~ 2,489)	195 ~ 205 (2,773 ~ 2,915)		165 ~ 175 (2,346 ~ 2,489)	195 ~ 205 (2,773 ~ 2,915)		165 ~ 175 (2,346 ~ 2,489)	195 ~ 205 (2,773 ~ 2,915)		165 ~ 175 (2,346 ~ 2,489)
4-1-(2)	Fuel injection pipe OD ϕ/ID ϕ x L	mm (in)	$\phi 6 / \phi 1.8 \times 400$ (0.2362/0.0708 x 15.748)		$\phi 6 / \phi 2 \times 600$ (0.2362/0.0787 x 23.622)	$\phi 6 / \phi 1.8 \times 400$ (0.2362/0.0708 x 15.748)		$\phi 6 / \phi 2 \times 600$ (0.2362/0.0787 x 23.622)	$\phi 6 / \phi 2 \times 400$ (0.2362/0.0787 x 15.748)		$\phi 6 / \phi 2 \times 600$ (0.2362/0.0787 x 23.622)	$\phi 6 / \phi 2 \times 400$ (0.2362/0.0787 x 15.748)		$\phi 6 / \phi 2 \times 600$ (0.2362/0.0787 x 23.622)
4-2	Top clearance /Prestroke	mm (in)	0.95 ~ 1.05/2.5 (0.0374 ~ 0.0413/0.0984)			0.95 ~ 1.05/2.5 (0.0374 ~ 0.0413/0.0984)			0.95 ~ 1.05/2.5 (0.0374 ~ 0.0413/0.0984)			0.95 ~ 1.05/2.5 (0.0374 ~ 0.0413/0.0984)		
4-7-1 Rated load	Pump rpm: N1	rpm	1,800			1,800			1,800			1,800		
	Rack position: R1	mm(in.)	7 (0.2756)			7 (0.2756)			7 (0.2756)			7 (0.2756)		
	Measuring stroke	St	1,000			1,000			1,000			1,000		
	Injection volume	cc	25		26.5 **27.5	31		32 **34	33		34 **36.5	40		47
	Nonuniformity	%	±3			±3			±3			±3		
4-7-2 No load	Pump rpm: N2	rpm	1,950			1,950			1,950			1,950		
	Rack position: R2	mm(in.)												
4-7-3 Idling	Pump rpm: N3	rpm	325			325			325			325		
	Measuring stroke	St	1,000			1,000			1,000			1,000		
	Injection volume	cc	7 ~ 8		8 ~ 9	9 ~ 10		10 ~ 11	9 ~ 10		10 ~ 11	9 ~ 10		10 ~ 11
	Nonuniformity	%	±10			±10			±10			±10		
4-7-4 Starting	Pump rpm: N4	rpm	200			200			200			200		
	Rack position	mm(in.)	11.5 ~ 12.5 (0.4527 ~ 0.4921)			11.5 ~ 12.5 (0.4527 ~ 0.4921)			11.5 ~ 12.5 (0.4527 ~ 0.4921)			11.5 ~ 12.5 (0.4527 ~ 0.4921)		
	Measuring stroke	St	1,000			1,000			1,000			1,000		
	Injection volume	cc	60 ~ 70		55 ~ 65, **65 ~ 75	60 ~ 70		55 ~ 65, **65 ~ 75	60 ~ 70		55 ~ 65, **65 ~ 75	60 ~ 70		65 ~ 75

NOTE 1: * Applicable engine number: #00575 and after (Engine model 4JHE)
NOTE 2: ** Applicable engine model and engine number: 4JH-TE #11001 and after
4JH-HTE #21001 and after
4JHE #01001 and after

Chapter 3 Fuel Injection Equipment
10. Tools

4JH Series

10. Tools

Name of tool	Shape and size	Application
Pump mounting scale for Yanmar tester 158090-51010 for Bosch (tester) 158090-51020		
Measuring device (cam backlash) 158090-51050		
Plunger insert 158090-51100		
Tappet holder 158090-51200		
Weight extractor 158090-51400		

Chapter 3 Fuel Injection Equipment
10. Tools — *4JH Series*

Name of tool	Shape and size	Application
Rack indicator 158090-51500		
Rack lock screw 158090-51010		
Dummy nut 158090-51520		
Nozzle plate 158090-51700		
Plunger gauge 121820-92540		
Top clearance gauge 158090-51300		
Timer extraction tool		

Chapter 3 Fuel Injection Equipment
11. Fuel Filter

4JH Series

11. Fuel Filter

The fuel filter is installed between the fuel feed pump and fuel injection pump, and removes dirt/foreign matter from the fuel pumped from the fuel tank.
The fuel filter element must be changed periodically. The fuel pumped by the fuel feed pump goes around the element, is fed through the pores in the filter and discharged from the center of the cover. Dirt and foreign matter in the fuel is deposited in the element.

11-1 Fuel filter specifications

Filtering method	filter paper
Filtering area	840cm² (130.20in.²)
Maximum flow	0.25 ℓ/min (15.25 in.³/min)
Pressure loss	100mm (3.9370in.) Hg or less
Max. dia. of unfiltered particle	5μ

11-2 Fuel filter inspection

The fuel strainer must be cleaned occasionally. If there is water or foreign matter in the strainer bowl, disassemble the strainer and wash with clean fuel oil to completely remove foreign matter. Replace the element every 300 hours of operation.
Replace the filter prior to this if the filter is very dirty, deformed or damaged.

Element changes	every 300 hours
Element part code number	129470-55700

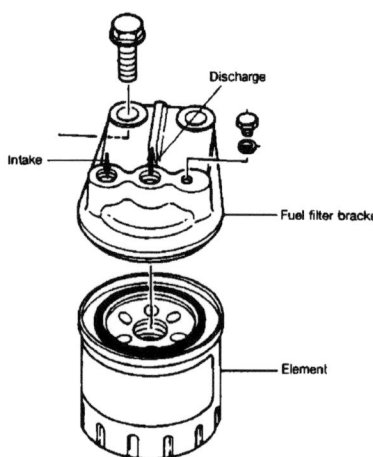

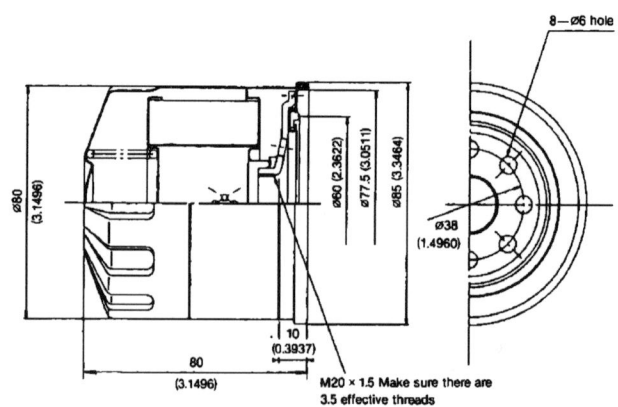

Printed in Japan
0000A0A1647

3-47

12. Fuel Tank

A triangular 30 liter fuel tank with a 2000mm (78.7402in.) rubber fuel hose to fit all models is available as an option. A fuel return connection is provided on top of the tank to which a rubber hose can be connected to return fuel from the fuel nozzles.

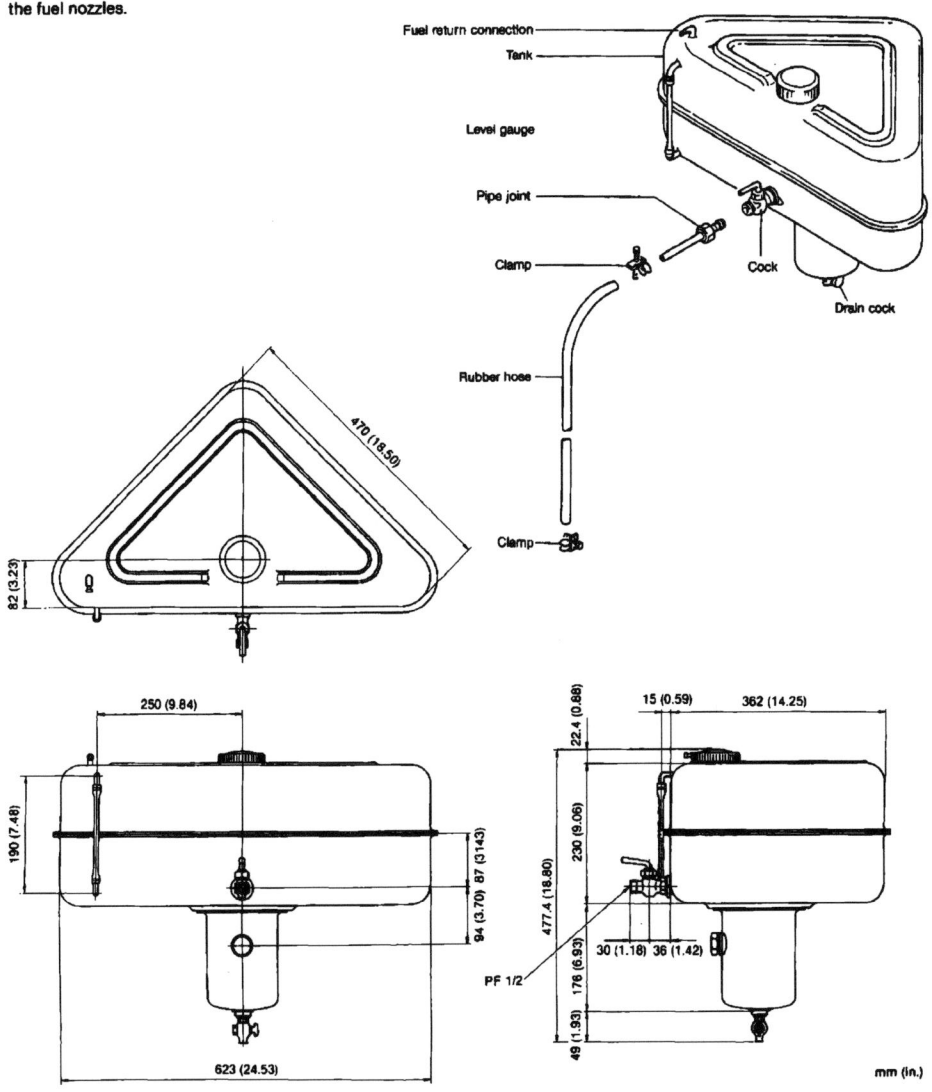

Chapter 3 Fuel Injection Equipment
13. Design Change of Fuel Piping Line

4JH Series

13. Design Change of Fuel Piping Line

To facility easy servicing, following design modifications will be made on the marine diesel engine model 4JH-series. Through the change of fuel piping line, air-bleeding will be done more easily.

13-1 Modification of fuel piping line.

13-2 Applicable engine models and serial numbers.

Engine Model	Serial Number	Plant Production
4JH(B)E	#01179 and thereafter	
4JH-T(B)E	#11201 and thereafter	From Dec., 1985
4JH-HT(B)E	#21226 and thereafter	
4JH-DT(B)E	#30312 and thereafter	

OLD FUEL PIPING LINE

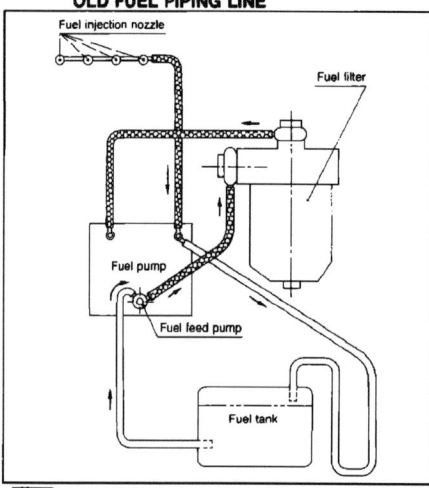

NEW FUEL PIPING LINE

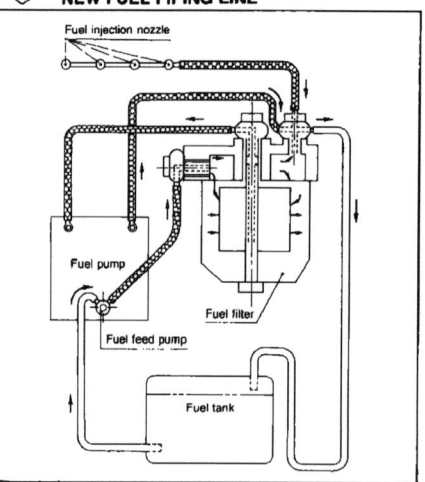

NOTE: Air-bleeding of the following engines with the modified fuel piping require the equivalent procedure as in the engine with the former fuel piping.

Engine Model	Serial Number
4JH(B)E	#01109 – 01178
4JH-T(B)E	#11143 – 11200
4JH-HT(B)E	#21180 – 21225
4JH-DT(B)E	#30256 – 30311

CHAPTER 4
INTAKE AND EXHAUST SYSTEM

 1. Intake and Exhaust System 4-1
 2. Intake Silencer 4-4
 3. Intake Manifold. 4-5
 4. Turbocharger 4-6
 5. Mixing Elbow 4-21
 6. Breather. 4-22